Exemplary Jews and Christians who became Sahabah

By Gregory Heary

The Sahabah are the Muslim companions of the Prophet Muhammad peace be upon him. A Sahabi is a singular male companion and a Sahabiyyat is a singular female companion. The Sahabah is the plural form of the word and includes both male and female companions. To be considered from among the Sahabah then someone had to be Muslim believing in the prophethood of Muhammad and meet Muhammad in person as a Muslim and lastly die as a Muslim. Many Jews and Christians set a wonderful example by recognizing the truth of Muhammad's prophetic religion and embraced Islam and met Muhammad in the flesh. This category of people are known as Ahl-Kitab Sahabah because they had previously believed in the previous Islamic prophets such as Moses and Jesus as well as books of divine revelation prior to meeting Muhammad and confirming his message as the God-given truth. These were the contemporary disciples of Muhammad who were Jews and Christians who met him and became Muslims.

For this book I cannot list all the Ahl-Kitab Sahabah because there are too many to count. So I have decided to include the most famous Jewish and Christian turned Muslim companions. After each one's biographical details I will include some of their most famously reported hadith that they narrated from the prophet. Also I have included a couple notables who became Muslims but due to circumstances did not meet Muhammad in person though they lived during his era, thus whilst not from the Sahabah they were still contemporaries of the prophet. Lastly after mentioning the males and females amongst this elite group I will include statements of Allah mentioned in the Quran about the Sahabah and Ahl-Kitab Sahabah. May God bless them all and guide us to follow in their exemplary footsteps to paradise.

Waraqa ibn Naufal

Waraqa bin Nawfal was the son of Khadija's paternal uncle. Khadija was the first wife of Muhammad (peace be upon him) and the first to believe in the prophethood of Muhammad (peace be upon him). Waraqa was one of the four men who left the pagan faith of Mecca in search for the Hanifite roots (the religion of Abraham (peace be upon him)) and returned as a devout learned Christian. He used to write and translate Scriptures.

The commencement of the Divine Inspiration to Allah's prophet began in the form of good righteous (true) dreams in his sleep. He never had a dream but that it came true exactly. Muhammad used to go in seclusion to the cave of Hira away from the polytheistic pagans of his hometown, where he used to worship God alone continuously for many nights. One day Divine Revelation descended upon him while he was in the cave of Hira. The angel came to him in it and asked him to read. The Prophet replied, "I do not know how to read." (The Prophet added), "The angel caught me (forcefully) and pressed me so hard that I could not bear it anymore. He then released me and again asked me to read, and I replied, "I do not know how to read," whereupon he caught me again and pressed me a second time till I could not bear it anymore. He then released me and asked me again to read, but again I replied, "I do not know how to read (or, what shall I read?)." Thereupon he caught me a third time and pressed me and then released me and said, *"Read! In the Name of your Lord, Who has created (all that exists), (1) He has created man from a clot (a piece of thick coagulated blood) (2) Read! And your Lord is the Most Generous, (3) Who has taught (the writing) by the pen. (4) He has taught man that which he knew not. (5)"* (Quran 96:1-5)

Then Allah's Prophet returned with the Inspiration, his neck muscles twitching with terror till he entered upon Khadija and said, "Cover me! Cover me!" She covered him till his fear was over and then he said, "O Khadija, what is wrong with me?" Then he told her everything that had happened and said, 'I fear that something may happen to me." Khadija said, 'Never! But have the glad tidings, for by Allah, Allah will never disgrace you as you keep good relations with your Kith and kin, speak the truth, help the poor and the destitute, serve your guest generously and assist the deserving, calamity-afflicted ones." Khadija then accompanied him to (her cousin) Waraqa bin Nawfal bin Asad bin 'Abdul 'Uzza bin Qusai. Waraqa was the son of her paternal uncle, i.e., her father's brother, who during the Pre-Islamic Period became a Christian and wrote the Gospels. He was an old man and had lost his eyesight. Khadija said to him, "O my cousin! Listen to the story of your nephew." Waraqa asked, "O my nephew! What have you seen?" The Prophet described what he had seen.

Waraqa said, "This is the same Namus (i.e., Gabriel, the Angel who keeps the secrets) whom Allah had sent to Moses. I wish I were young and could live up to the time when your people would turn you out." Allah's Prophet asked, "Will they turn me out?" Waraqa replied in the affirmative and said: "Never did a man come with something similar to what you have brought but was treated with hostility. If I should remain alive till the day when you will be turned out then I would support you strongly." But after a few days Waraqa died.

In a Daif hadith in Jami At-Tirmidhi 2288 Aishah said:

"The Messenger of Allah was asked about Waraqa. Khadijah said to him: 'He believed in you, but he died before your advent.' So the Messenger of Allah said: '*I saw him in a dream, and upon him were white garments. If he were among the inhabitants of the Fire then he would have been wearing other than that.*'"

Adaas

Adaas was a slave of Shiba bin Rabi'ah, from the inhabitants of the village of Ninevah from the area of Mosul. Adaas was Christian.

After the death of his uncle Abu Talib, Muhammad's ﷺ life was in danger in Mecca, so He ﷺ left for Taif with the hope of winning them over to Islam. After reaching Taif, He ﷺ visited the 3 chieftains of the clan separately, and placed before each of them the message of Allah. However instead of accepting his prophetic message, they refused to even listen to him, treating him in the most contemptuous and rude manner and ordered him to be expelled. Yet the polytheists wouldn't let him depart in peace, rather they set the mischievous street urchins after him, to hiss, to hoot, to jeer at and to stone him. He was pelted with stones that caused his whole body to be covered with blood, and his shoes were clogged with blood to his feet. Muhammad ﷺ left the town in this woeful plight. When he was away from the town, safe from the rabble, he prayed to Allah;

"O, Allah! To Thee I complain of the feebleness of my strength, of my lack of resources and my being unimportant in the eyes of people, O, Most Merciful of all those capable of showing mercy! Thou art the Lord of the weak, and Thou art my own Lord. To whom art Thou to entrust me; to an unsympathetic foe who would sullenly frown at me, or to an alien to whom Thou hast given control over my affairs? Not in the least do I care for anything except that I may have Thy protection for myself. I seek shelter in Your Light-the light which illuminates the Heavens and dispels all sorts of darkness, and which controls all affairs in this world as well as in the Hereafter. May it never be that I should incur Thy wrath, or that Thou should be displeased with me. I must remove the cause of Thy displeasure till Thou art pleased. There is no strength nor power but through Thee."

The Heavens were moved by the prayer and the angel Gabriel appeared before Muhammad ﷺ, greeting him with Assalamu'alaikum and said;

"Allah knows all that has passed between you and these people. He has deputed an angel in charge of the mountains to be at your command."

Saying this, Gabriel ushered the angel before the Prophet ﷺ. The angel greeted him and said;

"O, Prophet of Allah! I am at your service. If you wish, I can cause the mountains overlooking this town on both sides to collide with each other, so that all the people therein would be crushed to death, or you may suggest any other punishment for them."

Muhammad ﷺ said;

"Even if these people do not accept Islam, I do hope from Allah that there will be persons from among their progeny who would worship Allah and serve His cause."

During the prophet's return journey from Taif, Shiba and Utba, who were seeing the condition of Muhammad, sent their slave Addas to Muhammad with some grapes to eat. As Adaaas reached the Prophet ﷺ and presented the grapes, the Prophet ﷺ said Bismillah (in the name of God) and took them. Adaas said in surprise, "I am hearing a new style of speech. By Allah! The people of this area do not say such words." (since it was unlike the polytheistic practices of his owners) Muhammad said, "Where do you live? What is your religion?" Adaas said, "I am a Christian resident of Nineveh." The Prophet said, "You are from the town of the pious man Yunus(Jonah) bin Matta." Adaas said, "How did you know who Yunus (Jonah) is?" The Prophet ﷺ said " He is my brother. He was a Prophet, and I am also a Prophet."

Adaas saw these signs and attributes of prophethood and kissed his blessed hands, and feet and said:

. اشهد انک عبد الله ورسوله

"Ishahad Ink Abdullah Wa Rassulah"

"I bear witness that indeed you belong to Allah's servants and His messengers."

Shiba and Utba were watching this encounter of Adaas from afar and when he returned, they asked him why Adaas kissed his hand, Adaas said " O my Master! There is no person on this earth better than that man. He told me things that only a prophet could know." after hearing this both of them told Adaas that he should not turn you away from your religion.

On the day of the battle of Badr, when both sides were preparing for war, Adaas sat on a mound, when Shiba and Rabi'ah passed by, he held their feet and said, "By God, you people are going to fight the Prophet. It is very difficult for you to come back." Adaas had a close relationship with both Shiba and Rabi'ah, so he explained many things about Islamic truth to them, but when they refused to agree, Adaas disassociated from them. Adaas was killed during the Battle of Badr.

Abdullah bin Salam

Abdullah bin Salam was a Jewish Scholar and Rabbi biologically descended from prophet Joseph, and thus by extension also from the lineage of prophets Jacob, Isaac and Abraham pbut. Prior to becoming Muslim his name was Hussain. Abdullah bin Salam's story is as follows:

"When I heard of the Messenger of Allah, I recognized his attributes, his name, and the time he would appear, which all coincided with our books. When he arrived in Medinah, a man informed me of his arrival while I was on top of my date palm tree. I shouted 'Allah is the Greatest!' My aunt was sitting beneath me and said " By Allah, if you had heard that Moses was coming you would not have been more enthusiastic." I said to her "O auntie, I swear by Allah, he is the brother of Moses who has been sent." My aunt said ' Is he the prophet that we were informed would appear during this time?' I said: "Yes." She said, "So be it." Upon the spot my aunt Khalidah bint al Harith embraced Islam as did my household.

After the Messenger of Allah arrived in Medinah I went to meet him and investigate his claim to prophecy. Upon gazing at the face of the Messenger of Allah I knew his face was not the face of a liar. The first thing the prophet said to the people was:

O people, spread the greeting of salam, give food to the poor, and perform the prayer while the people are sleeping. You will enter paradise with safety and security.

When meeting the prophet Abdullah bin Salam said, "I will ask you about three things which nobody knows unless he be a prophet. Firstly, what is the first portent of the Hour? What is the first meal of the people of Paradise? And what makes a baby look like its father or mother?'. The Prophet (ﷺ) said, "Just now Gabriel has informed me about that." `Abdullah said, "Gabriel?" The Prophet (ﷺ) said, "Yes." `Abdullah said, "He, among the angels is the enemy of the Jews." On that the Prophet (ﷺ) recited this Quranic Verse:-- "Whoever is an enemy to Gabriel (let him die in his fury!) for he has brought it (i.e. Qur'an) down to your heart by Allah's permission." (2.97) Then he added, "As for the first portent of the Hour, it will be a fire that will collect the people from the East to West. And as for the first meal of the people of Paradise, it will be the caudite (i.e.

extra) lobe of the fish liver. And if a man's discharge proceeded that of the woman, then the child resembles the father, and if the woman's discharge proceeded that of the man, then the child resembles the mother." After hearing these correct answers, `Abdullah said, "I testify that None has the right to be worshipped but Allah, and that you are the Messenger of Allah and that you have come with the Truth."

Then Abdullah bin Salam said: "The Jews know well that I am their chief, and the son of their chief, and the most learned amongst them, and the son of the most learned amongst them. So send for them and ask them about me before they know I have embraced Islam. For if they know that, they will say things about me that are not correct." So the Messenger of Allah sent for the Jews and they came while Abdullah bin Salam hid. The Messenger of Allah said to them, "O Jews, woe to you, fear Allah. By Allah, the One whom no one deserves to be worshipped except for Him, you people know for certain that I am the Messenger of Allah and that I have come to you with the truth, so embrace Islam." The Jews replied, "We do not know this." The prophet repeated his statement three times and the Jews replied the same three times. Then the prophet said, "What kind of man is ibn Salam amongst you?" The Jews said, 'He is our chief, and the son of our chief, and the most learned man, and the son of the most learned amongst us.'

The prophet then said, "What would you think if he should embrace Islam?" The Jews said: "Allah forbid! He cannot embrace Islam." The prophet said, "What would you think if he should embrace Islam?" The Jews again replied, 'Allah forbid! He cannot embrace Islam. So the prophet called out "O Ibn Salam! Come out to them." So Ibn Salam came out from his hidden place and said "O Jews! Fear Allah, the One whom no one deserves to be worshipped except for Him. You know for certain that he is the Messenger of Allah and that he has brought the true religion! I testify that None has the right to be worshipped but Allah and that Muhammad is the Messenger of Allah." The Jews responded, "You tell a lie." The Jews then proclaimed, "He is the worst of us and the son of the worst of us!" In reply Abdullah bin Salam said, "O Allah's Messenger (ﷺ)! This is what I was afraid of!"

It was narrated that Abdullah bin Salam said:

"I came to the Messenger of Allah, and my name was not Abdullah bin Salam. The Messenger of Allah named me Abdullah bin Salam."

Source: Sunan Ibn Majah 3734 Grade: Daif

Narrated 'Abdullah bin Salam:

"The description of Muhammad is written in the Tawrah, [and the description that] 'Eisa(Jesus) will be buried next to him."

Source: Jami` at-Tirmidhi 3617 Grade: Hasan

It was narrated from 'Abdullah bin Salam that he heard the Messenger of Allah (ﷺ) saying on the pulpit one Friday:

"There is nothing wrong with anyone of you buying two garments for Friday (prayer), other than his daily work clothes."

Source: Sunan Ibn Majah 1095 Grade: Hasan

Narrated Abu Hurairah:

The Messenger of Allah said: The best day on which the sun has risen is Friday; on it Adam was created, on it he was expelled (from Paradise), on it his contrition was accepted, on it he died, and on it the Last Hour will take place. On Friday every beast is on the lookout from dawn to sunrise in fear of the Last Hour, but not jinn and men, and it contains a time at which no Muslim prays and asks anything from Allah but He will give it to him. Ka'b said: That is one day every year. So I said: It is on every Friday. Ka'b read the Torah and said: The Messenger of Allah has spoken the truth. Abu Hurairah said: I met Abdullah ibn Salam and told him of my meeting with Ka'b. Abdullah ibn Salam said: I know what time it is.

Abu Hurairah said: I asked him to tell me about it. Abdullah ibn Salam said: It is at the very end of Friday. I asked: How can it be when the Messenger of Allah has said: "No Muslim finds it while he is praying...." and this is the moment when no prayer is offered. Abdullah ibn Salam said: Has the Messenger of Allah not said: "If anyone is seated waiting for the prayer, he is engaged in the prayer until he observes it." I said: Yes, it is so.

Source: Sunan Abi Dawud 1046 Grade: Sahih

Dawud ibn Abi Dawud said,

"'Abdullah ibn Salam said to me, 'If you hear that the Dajjal(Anti-christ) has come out while you are planting young palm trees, it is not too late to plant it, for people will still have livelihood after that."

Source: Al Adab al Mufrad Grade: Daif

Narrated Qais bin 'Ubada:

I was sitting in a gathering in which there was Sa`d bin Malik and Ibn `Umar. `Abdullah bin Salam passed in front of them and they said, "This man is from the people of Paradise." I said to `Abdullah bin Salam, "They said so-and-so." He replied, "Subhan Allah! They ought not to have said things of which they have no knowledge, but I saw (in a dream) that a post was fixed in a green garden. At the top of the post there was a handhold and below it there was a servant. I was asked to climb (the post). So I climbed it till I got hold of the handhold." Then I narrated this dream to Allah's Messenger. Allah's Apostle said, "`Abdullah will die while still holding the firm reliable handhold (i.e., Islam).

Source: Sahih Bukhari 7010

Narrated `Abdullah bin Salam:

(In a dream) I saw myself in a garden, and there was a pillar in the middle of the garden, and there was a handhold at the top of the pillar. I was asked to climb it. I said, "I cannot." Then a servant came and lifted up my clothes and I climbed (the pillar), and then got hold of the handhold, and I

woke up while still holding it. I narrated that to the Prophet who said, "The garden symbolizes the garden of Islam, and the handhold is the firm Islamic handhold which indicates that you will be adhering firmly to Islam until you die."

Source: Sahih al-Bukhari 7014

Abdullah bin Salam said:

"A group of us Companions of the Messenger of Allah sat talking, and we said: 'If we knew which deed was most beloved to Alllah then we would do it.' So Allah, Most High, revealed: Whatsoever is in the heavens and whatsoever is on the earth glorifies Allah. And He is Almighty, the All-Wise. O you who believe! Why do you say that which you do not do?" Abdullah bin Salam said: "So the Messenger of Allah recited it to us."

Source: Jami` at-Tirmidhi 3309 Grade: Sahih

Narrated Abu Burda:

When I arrived at Medina, `Abdullah bin Salam met me and said to me, "Accompany me to my house so that I may make you drink from a bowl from which Allah's Messenger used to drink, and that you may offer prayer in the mosque in which the Prophet used to pray." I accompanied him, and he made me drink Sawiq and gave me dates to eat, and then I prayed in his mosque.

Source: Sahih al-Bukhari 7342

Narrated Abu Burda:

When I came to Medina. I met `Abdullah bin Salam. He said, "Will you come to me so that I may serve you with Sawiq (i.e. powdered barley) and dates, and let you enter a (blessed) house that in which the Prophet entered?" Then he added, "You are in a country where the practice of Riba (i.e. usury) is prevalent; so if somebody owe you something and he sends you a present of a load of chopped straw or a load of barley or a load of provender then do not take it, as it is Riba."

Source: Sahih al-Bukhari 3814

Narrated `Abdullah bin `Umar:

The Jews came to Allah's Messenger and told him that a man and a woman from amongst them had committed illegal sexual intercourse. Allah's Messenger said to them, "What do you find in the Torah about the legal punishment of Ar-Rajm (stoning)?" They replied, (But) we announce their crime and lash them." `Abdullah bin Salam said, "You are telling a lie; Torah contains the order of Rajm." They brought and opened the Torah and one of them solaced his hand on the Verse of Rajm and read the verses preceding and following it. `Abdullah bin Salam said to him, "Lift your hand." When he lifted his hand, the Verse of Rajm was written there. They said, "Muhammad has told the truth; the Torah has the Verse of Rajm. The Prophet then gave the order that both of them should be stoned to death. `Abdullah bin `Umar said, "I saw the man leaning over the woman to shelter her from the stones."

Source: Sahih al-Bukhari 3635

Narrated Yazid bin 'Umairah:

"When death was upon Mu'adh bin Jabal, it was said to him: 'O Abu 'Abdur-Rahman, advise us.' He said: 'Sit me up.' So he said: 'Indeed, knowledge and faith are at their place, whoever desires them shall find them.' He said that three times. 'And seek knowledge from four men: 'Uwaimir Abu Ad-Darda, with Salman Al-Farisi, with 'Abdullah bin Mas'ud, and with 'Abdullah bin Salam who used to be a Jew and then accepted Islam. For indeed, I heard the Messenger of Allah saying, "Indeed he is the tenth of ten in Paradise."

Source: Jami` at-Tirmidhi 3804 Grade: Sahih

Narrated 'Abdul-Malik bin 'Umair:

from the nephew of 'Abdullah bin Salam who said: "When they were after 'Uthman, 'Abdullah bin Salam came, and 'Uthman said to him: 'What did you come for?' He said: 'I came to assist you.' He said: 'Go to the people to repel their advances against me. For verily your going is better to me than your entering here.'" He said: "So 'Abdullah bin Salam went to the people and said: 'O you people! During Jahiliyyah I was named so-and-so, then the Messenger of Allah named me 'Abdullah, and some Ayat from the Book of Allah were revealed about me. (The following) was revealed about me: 'A witness from among the Children of Isra'il has testified to something similar, and believed while you rejected. Verily, Allah does not guide the wrongdoing people. (46:10)" And (the following) was revealed about me: 'Sufficient as a witness between me and you is Allah, and those too who have knowledge of the Scripture. (13:43)" Allah has sheathed the sword from you and the angels are your neighbors in this city of yours, the one in which the Revelation came to your Prophet. But by Allah! (Fear) Allah regarding this man(Uthman); if you kill him, then by Allah! If you kill him, then you will cause the angels to remove your goodness from you, and to raise Allah's sheathed sword against you, such that it will never be sheathed again until the Day of Resurrection.'" He said: "They said: 'Kill the Jew and kill 'Uthman.'"

Source: Jami` at-Tirmidhi 3256 Grade: Daif

Abdullah bin Salam died in Medinah during the Caliphate of Muawwiya.

Salamah ibn Salam the Israeli

Salamah ibn Salam was either the brother or nephew of the previously mentioned Abdullah bin Salam. He was a Jew prior to embracing Islam hence the addendum to his name "the Israeli".

Salma bin Salam

His father was Salamah ibn Salam the Israeli and he was also Jewish prior to embracing Islam.

Salman Farsi

His original name and ancestry was Mabah ibn Bozahshan bin Mor Salan bin Yahozaan bin Feroze ibn Sahrik. It was only after Islam that his name changed from Mabah to Salman. The father of Salman was a resident of an area in Isbahan. His father loved Salman so much that he used to forbid him from leaving the house out of concern for his safety. Salman was zealous for religion since his childhood and developed a very deep interest in fire worshipping as his family brought him up to be Zoroastrian. He became ascetic and used to look after the fire day and night to the extent that he was among those elite Zoroastrian worshippers who were responsible for keeping the fire lit. Abdullah ibn Abbas narrated Salman Farsi's story as he heard it from Salman:

"I was a Persian man, one of the people of Isbahan, from a village called Jayy. My father was the chief of his village, and I was the dearest of Allah's creation to him. He loved me so much that he kept me in his house near the fire, just like where the girls are kept. I strove hard in the Magian religion until I became the keeper of the fire, which I tended and did not let go out for a moment. My father had a huge garden, and he was busy one day with some construction work, so he said, 'O my son, I am too busy with this building today, go and check my garden,' and he told me some of the things he wanted done. I went out, heading toward his garden, and I passed by one of the Christian churches where I could hear their voices as they were praying. I did not know anything about the people, because my father had kept me in his house. When I passed by and heard their voices, I entered upon them to see what they were doing. When I saw them, I was impressed with their prayer, and I was attracted to their way. I said "By Allah, this is better than the religion that we follow." By Allah I did not leave them until the sun set, and I forgot about my father's garden and did not go there.

I said to them, 'Where did this religion originate?' They said, 'In Syria.' Then I went back to my father, who had sent people out to look for me, and I had distracted him from all his work. When I came to him he said, 'O my son where were you? Did I not ask you to do what I asked?' I said, 'O my father, I passed by some people who were praying in a church, and I was impressed with what I saw of their religion. By Allah, I stayed with them until the sun set.' He said, 'O my son, there is nothing good in that religion. Your religion and the religion of your forefathers is better than that.' I said, 'No, by Allah, it is better than our religion.' He was afraid for me, and he put fetters on my legs and kept me in his house. I sent word to the Christians, saying, 'If any Christian merchants come to you from Syria, tell me about them.' He said, "Some Christian merchants came to them from Syria, and they told me about them. I said to them, 'When they have completed their business and want to go back to their own country, tell me about that.' So when they wanted to go back to their own country, they told me about that, and I threw off the irons from my legs and went out with them, until I came to Syria.

When I reached Syria, I said, 'Who is the best person in this religion?' They said, "The bishop in the church." So I went to him and said, 'I like this religion, and I would like to stay with you and serve you in your church , and learn from you and pray with you.' He said, 'Come in.' So I went in with him, but he was a bad man. He would command them and exhort them to give charity, but he kept a great deal of wealth for himself and did not give it to the poor. He had amassed seven chests of gold and silver. I hated him deeply when I saw what he was doing. Then he died and the Christians gathered to bury him. I said to them, "This was a bad man. He commanded you and exhorted you to give charity, but when you brought it to him he kept it for himself and did not give any of it to the poor." They said, 'How do you know that? Show us where his treasure is.' So I showed them where it was and they brought out seven chests filled with gold and silver. When they saw that they said, 'By Allah, we will never bury him.' Then they crucified him and pelted him with stones. Then they brought another man and appointed him in his place.' Salman said, "I have never seen a man who does not offer the five daily prayers who was better than him. He shunned this world and sought the Hereafter, and no one strove harder than him night and day. I loved him as I had never loved anyone before and I stayed with him for a while.

When he was about to die, I said, 'O so and so, I was with you and I loved you as I had never loved anyone before, and now the decree of Allah has come to you as you see. To whom do you advise me to go? What do you command me to do?' He said, "O my son, by Allah, I do not know of anyone today who follows what I followed. The people are doomed. They have changed and abandoned most of what they used to follow, except for a man in Mosul, Iraq. He is so and so, and he follows what I used to follow, so go and join him."

When he died and was buried, I went to the man in Mosul. I said to him, 'O so and so, so and so advised me when he died to come to you and he told me that you follow the same religion as he followed.' He said to me, 'Stay with me.' So I stayed with him, and I found him to be a good man who followed the same religion as his companion had followed. But soon he died. When he was dying, I said to him, 'O so and so, I was advised to come to you and told to join you, but now there has come to you from Allah what you see. To whom do you advise me to go? What do you command me to do?' He said, "O my son, by Allah I do not know of anyone who follows what we used to follow except a man in Nusaybin. He is so and so. Go to him."

When he died and was buried, I went to the man in Nusaybin. I came to him and told him my story and what my companion had told me to do. He said, "Stay with me." So I stayed with him and I found him to be a follower of the same religion as his two companions, and he was a good man. By Allah, soon death came upon him and when he was dying, I said to him, 'O so and so, so and so advised me to go to so and so. Then so and so advised me to come to you. To whom do you advise me to go and what do you command me to do?' He said, "O my son, by Allah, we do not know of anyone left who follows our way and to whom I can tell you to go except a man in Amorium. He follows something like what we follow. If you wish go to him, for he follows our way."

When he died and was buried, I went to the man in Amorium and told him my story. He said, "Stay with me." So I stayed with a man who was following the same as his companions. I earned wealth until I had cows and sheep, then the decree of Allah came to him. When he was dying, I said to him, 'O so and so, I was with so and so, and so and so told me to go to so and so. Then so and so told me to go to so and so; then so and so told me to come to you. To whom do you advise me to go and what do you command me to do?' He said, "O my son, by Allah, I do not know of anyone who follows our way to whom I can advise you to go. But there has come the time of a Prophet, who will be sent with the religion of Abraham. He will appear in the land of the Arabs and will migrate to a land between two lands with black rocks, between which there are palm trees. He will have characteristics that will not be hidden. He will eat of what is given as a gift, but he will not eat of what is given as charity. Between his shoulder blades is the Seal of Prophethood. If you can go to that land then do so.'

Then he died and was buried, and I stayed in Amorium as long as Allah willed I should stay. Then some merchants of Kalb tribe passed by me, and I said to them, 'Will you take me to the land of the Arabs, and I will give you these cows and sheep of mine?' They said, 'Yes.' So I gave them the cows and sheep, and they took me there. But when they brought me to the valley of al-Qura, they wronged me and sold me as a slave to a Jewish man. When I was with him, I saw the palm trees, and I hoped that this was the land that my companion had described to me, but I was not sure. While I was with him, a cousin of his from Banu Qurayzah came to him from Madinah, and he sold me to him and he took me to Madinah. By Allah, as soon as I saw it, I recognized it from the description given to me by my companion. I stayed there and Allah sent His Messenger, who stayed in Mecca as long as he stayed, and I did not hear anything about him because I was so busy with the work of a slave. Then he migrated to Madinah, and by Allah, I was at the top of a palm tree belonging to my master, doing some work on it, and my master was sitting there. Then a cousin of his came and stood beside him and said, 'May Allah kill Banu Qayla! By Allah, right now they are gathering in Quba to welcome a man who has come from Mecca today, and they say that he is a prophet.'

When I heard that, I began to shiver so much that I thought I would fall on top of my master. I came down from the tree and started saying to that cousin of his, 'What are you saying, what are you saying?' My master got angry, and he struck me with his fist and said, 'What has it got to do with you? Go back to your work!' I said, 'Nothing, I just wanted to make sure of what he was saying.' I had something that I had collected, and when evening came, I went to the Messenger of Allah when he was in Quba and I entered upon him and said to him, 'I have heard that you are a righteous man, and that you have Companions who are strangers and are in need. This is something that I have to give in charity, and I see that you are more in need of it than anyone else.' I brought it near to him, and the Messenger of Allah said to his Companions, "Eat." But he refrained from eating. I said to myself, 'This is one.'

Then I went away and collected some more. The Messenger of Allah went to Madinah, then I came to him and said, 'I see that you do not eat food given in charity. This is a gift with which I wish to honor you.' The Messenger of Allah ate some of it and told his Companions to eat too. I said to myself, 'This is two.'

Then I came to the Messenger of Allah when he was in Baqee al-Gharqad, where he had attended the funeral of one of his Companions. I greeted him with the greeting of salam then I moved behind him, trying to look at his back to see the seal that my companion had described to me. When the Messenger of Allah saw me going behind him, he realized that I was trying to find confirmation of something that had been described to me, so he let his cloak drop from his back, and I saw the seal and recognized it. Then I embraced him, kissing the seal and weeping. The Messenger of Allah said to me, "Turn around." So I turned around and I told him my story as I have told it to you, O Ibn Abbas."

The Messenger of Allah wanted his companions to hear that. Then Salman was kept busy with the work of a slave, until he had missed the Battle of Badr and Uhud. He said, "Then the Messenger of Allah said to me, Draw up a contract of manumission, O Salman." So I drew up a contract of manumission with my master in return for 300 palm trees which I would plant for him, and 40 uqiyahs. The Messenger of Allah said to his Companions, 'Help your brother.' So they helped me with the palm trees, one man gave 30 small trees and another gave 20, and another gave 15, and another gave 10, each man gave according to what he had, until they had collected 300 small trees for me. Then the Messenger of Allah said to me, 'Go, O Salman, and dig the holes where they are to be planted. When you have finished, come to me and I will plant them with my own hand.' So I dug the holes for them, and my companions helped me, then when I had finished, I came to him and told him. The Messenger of Allah came out with me and we started to bring the trees close, and the Messenger of Allah planted the trees with his own hand.

By the One in whose hand is the soul of Salman, not one single tree among them died. So I had paid off the trees but there still remained the money. A piece of gold the size of an egg was brought to the Messenger of Allah from one of his military campaigns. He said, "What happened to the Persian who had a contract of manumission?" I was summoned to him and he said, "Take this and pay off what you owe, O Salman." I said, 'How could this pay off everything I owe, O Messenger of Allah?' He said, 'Take it, and Allah will help you to pay off what you owe.' So I took it and weighed it for them and by the One in whose hand is the soul of Salman, it was 40 uqiyahs, so I paid them their dues and I was set free. I was present with the Messenger of Allah at the Battle of the Trench, and after that I did not miss any major event with him."

The prophet assigned Salman Farsi to be brothers with Abu-Darda.

During the Battle of the Trench, where over 10,000 polytheists fought against the 3,000 Muslims besieged in Medinah, it is reported that Salman Farsi was the person who suggested a trench be dug; as he was familiar with Persian trench warfare. It took 6 entire days for the trenches to be dug. Yet this non-Arabian tactic surprised and stopped the disbelievers in their tracks until they eventually retreated weeks later unable to break through the trenches the Muslims dug.

Ali said about Salman, "*He knows the first knowledge (i.e. of the previous revealed books) and the last one (i.e. the Quran and the Sunnah); he is a sea (of knowledge) that is very deep to the extent that you cannot reach its bottom; he is from us the family of the household [of the Prophet].*" [Reported by Ibn Abu Shaybah, Ibn Sa'd and others]

During the caliphate of Umar, Salman became the Governor of Madain. At the time of Salman's death, 20 or 22 Dirhams amounted to his entire net worth. He used to cry on account of this too and used to say that the Prophet said that a person's equipment should not be more than a traveler, and this is my condition. This condition remained constant throughout his life, even when he was distinguished in the position of governing. Hasan narrates that when Salman was getting a salary of 5,000 and was ruling over 1,000 souls, he only had one Abaya which he used to collect wood, lay half of it, and cover half of it. He used to ride a donkey, remain undistinguishable from the poor and count the pieces of meat to the servant so that no suspicion would arise on his part. Salman would buy palm leaves for one dirham and weave them, then he would sell the product for three dirhams and spend them in the following manner: one dirham to buy more palm leaves, one dirham for his family and one dirham to be given in charity.

Narrated Salman:

The interval between Jesus and Muhammad was six hundred years.

Source: Sahih al-Bukhari 3948

Salman said:

"The people of correctness in this world are the people of correctness in the Next World."

Source: Al-Adab Al-Mufrad 223

Narrated Abu Juhaifa:

The Prophet established a bond of brotherhood between Salman and Abu Darda'. Salman paid a visit to Abu ad-Darda and found Um Ad-Darda' dressed in shabby clothes and asked her why she was in that state.?" She replied, "Your brother, Abu Ad-Darda is not interested in the luxuries of this world." In the meantime Abu Ad-Darda came and prepared a meal for him (Salman), and said to him, "(Please) eat for I am fasting." Salman said, "I am not going to eat, unless you eat." So Abu Ad-Darda' ate. When it was night, Abu Ad-Darda' got up (for the night prayer). Salman said (to him), "Sleep," and he slept. Again Abu- Ad-Darda' got up (for the prayer), and Salman said (to him), "Sleep." When it was the last part of the night, Salman said to him, "Get up now (for the prayer)." So both of them offered their prayers and Salman said to Abu Ad-Darda',"Your Lord has a right on you; and your soul has a right on you; and your family has a right on you; so you should give the rights of all those who have a right on you). Later on Abu Ad-Darda' visited the Prophet and mentioned that to him. The Prophet, said, "Salman has spoken the truth."

Source: Sahih al-Bukhari 6139

Narrated Salman:

"The Messenger of Allah said to me: 'O Salman! Do not detest me and thereby leave your religion.' I said: 'O Messenger of Allah! How could I detest you while Allah guided us by you.' He said: 'You will detest the Arabs and thereby detest me.'"

Source: Jami` at-Tirmidhi 3927 Grade: Daif

Narrated Salman al-Farsi:

It was said to Salman: Your Prophet teaches you everything, even about excrement. He replied: Yes. He has forbidden us to face the qiblah at the time of easing or urinating, and cleansing with right hand, and cleansing with less than three stones, or cleansing with dung or bone.

Source: Sunan Abi Dawud 7 Grade: Sahih

Narrated Salman al-Farsi:

The Prophet said: Your Lord is munificent and generous, and is ashamed to turn away empty the hands of His servant when he raises them to Him.

Source: Sunan Abi Dawud 1488 Grade: Sahih

Narrated Abu Hurairah:

"Some people among the Companions of the Messenger of Allah said: 'O Messenger of Allah! Who are these people whom Allah mentioned, that if we turn away they would replace us, then they would not be like us?'" He said: "And Salman was beside the Messenger of Allah, so the Messenger of Allah patted Salman's thigh and said: 'This one and his companions, and by the One in Whose Hand is my soul! If faith were suspended from Pleiades, then it would be reached by men from Persia.'"

Source: Jami` at-Tirmidhi 3261 Grade: Hasan

Umm ad-Darda' said,

"Salman came from al-Mada'in (Ctesiphon) to Syria to visit us on foot wearing a shirt (kisa') and trousers." Shawdhab said, "Salman was seen wearing a short with all his hair shaved off and his large ears showing. He was told, 'You have made yourself ugly.' He replied, "The real good is the good of the Next World.'"

Source: Al-Adab Al-Mufrad 346 Grade: Hasan

Salman Farisi reported Allah's Messenger (ﷺ) as saying:

Verily, there are one hundred (parts of) mercy for Allah, and it is one part of this mercy by virtue of which there is mutual love between the people and ninety-nine reserved for the Day of Resurrection.

Source: Sahih Muslim 2753a

Salman Al-Farisi said:

The Prophet said, "Do not, if you can help, be the first to enter the market and the last to leave it because it is an arena of Satan and the standard of Satan is set there."

Source: Riyad as-Salihin 1842 and Sahih Muslim

It was narrated that Salman said:

"The Messenger of Allah said to me: 'There is no man who purifies himself on Friday as he is commanded, then comes out of his house to the

Friday prayer, and listens attentively until he finishes his prayer, but it will be an expiation for what came before it the week before."

Source: Sunan an-Nasa'i 1403 Grade: Sahih

It was narrated from Thabit that Anas said:

"Salman felt sick and Sa'd came to visit him, and when he saw him he wept. Sa'd said to him: 'Why are you weeping, my brother? Are you not a Companion of the Messenger of Allah? Are you not? Are you not?' Salman said: 'I am only weeping for one reason: I am not weeping because of longing for this world or for dislike of the Hereafter. But the Messenger of Allah gave me some advice and I think that I have transgressed.' He said: 'What was his advice to you?' He said: 'He advised me that something like the provision of a rider is sufficient for anyone of you, and I think that I have transgressed that. As for you, O Sa'd, fear Allah when you pass a verdict, and when you distribute (spoils of war), and when you decide to do anything.'"

Source: Sunan Ibn Majah 4104 Grade: Hasan

It has been narrated on the authority of Salman who said:

I heard the Messenger of Allah say: Keeping watch for a day and a night is better (in point of reward) than fasting for a whole month and standing in prayer every night. If a person dies (while, performing this duty), his (meritorious) activity will continue and he will go on receiving his reward for it perpetually and will be saved from the torture of the grave.

Source: Sahih Muslim 1913a

Salman reported that Allah's Messenger (ﷺ) said:

Verily, Allah created, on the same very day when He created the heavens and the earth, one hundred parts of mercy. Every part of mercy is coextensive with the space between the heavens. and the earth and He out of this mercy endowed one part to the earth and it is because of this that the mother shows affection to her child and even the beasts and birds show kindness to one another and when there would be the Day of Resurrection, Allah would make full (use of Mercy).

Source: Sahih Muslim 2753c

Narrated Buraidah:

that the Messenger of Allah said: "Indeed Allah has ordered me to love four, and He informed me that He loves them." It was said: "O Messenger of Allah! Name them for us." He said: "'Ali is among them," saying that three times, "And Abu Dharr, Al-Miqdad, and Salman. And He ordered me to love them, and He informed me that He loves them."

Source: Jami` at-Tirmidhi 3718 Grade: Daif

Salman al-Farisi reported:

God's messenger saying in a sermon which he delivered to them on the last day of Sha'ban, "A great month, a blessed month, a month containing a night which is better than a thousand months has approached you people. God has appointed the observance of fasting during it as an obligatory duty, and the passing of its night in prayer as a voluntary practice. If someone draws near to God during it with some good act he will be like one who fulfils an obligatory duty in another month, and he who fulfills an obligatory duty in it will be like one who fulfills seventy obligatory duties in another month. It is the month of endurance, and the reward of endurance is paradise. It is the month of sharing with others, and a month in which the believer's provision is increased. If someone gives one who has been fasting something with which to break his fast it will provide forgiveness of his sins and save him from hell, and he will have a reward equal to his without his reward being diminished in any respect." Some of them remarked to God's messenger that they did not all have the means to give one who had been fasting something with which to break his fast, and he replied, "God gives this reward to him who gives one who has been fasting some milk mixed with water, or a date, or a drink of water with which to break his fast, and anyone who gives a full meal to one who has been fasting will be given a drink from any tank by God and will not thirst till he enters paradise. It is a month whose beginning is mercy, whose middle is forgiveness, and whose end is freedom from hell. If anyone makes things easy for his slave during it, God will forgive him and free him from hell."

Source: Mishkat al-Masabih 1965

Narrated Abu Al-Bakhtari:

"*An Army from the armies of the Muslims, whose commander was Salman Al-Farisi, besieged one of the Persian castles. They said: 'O Abu 'Abdullah! Should we charge them?' He said: 'Leave me to call them (to Islam) as I heard the Messenger of Allah call them.' So Salman went to them and said: 'I am only a man from among you, a Persian, and you see that the Arabs obey me. If you become Muslims then you will have the likes of what we have, and from you will be required that which is required from us. If you refuse, and keep your religion, then we will leave you to it, and you will give us the Jizyah from your hands while you are submissive.' He said to them in Persian: 'And you are other than praiseworthy and if you refuse then we will equally resist you.' They said: 'We will not give you the Jizyah, we will fight you instead.' So they said: 'O Abu 'Abdullah! Should we charge them?' He said: 'No.'*" He said: "*So for three days he called them to the same (things), and then he said: 'Charge them.'*" He said: "*So we charged them, and we conquered the castle.*"

Source: Jami` at-Tirmidhi 1548 Grade: Daif

Abdu'r-Rahman ibn Sa'id reported that his father said:

"*I was with Salman when he visited a sick person in Kinda. When he went in, he said, 'Good news! Allah makes the illness of the believer an expiation for him and a restoration, whereas the illness of the corrupt person is like a camel whose people hobble it and the let it go. It does not know why it was hobbled or released.'*"

Source: Al-Adab Al-Mufrad 493

Salman al Farsi said:

"Knowledge is plentiful while life is short. So seek knowledge which you will need in matters of your religion and leave aside all else – do not spend your efforts in learning it."

Salman al Farsi said:

"I love to eat from the earnings of my hands."

Salman al Farsi said:

"Those with the most sins on the day of Resurrection will be those who speak the most in matters concerning disobedience to Allah."

Jarir narrated he had a conversation with Salman al Farsi and Salman said:

"O Jarir! Humble yourself for Allah's sake because the one who humbles himself for His sake in this world, Allah will elevate him in the hereafter. O Jarir! Do you know what is the cause of darkness on the day of Resurrection?"

Jarir replied: "No"

Salman said: "People oppressing and wronging each other in this world."

Salman then took a small twig which Jarir could barely see between his fingers and said: "O Jarir! If you were to look for a twig like this in Paradise you will not find it."

Jarir said: "What about the date palms and trees [of Paradise]?

Salman said: "Their roots and bases will be of pearls and gold, and their crests will be laden with fruit."

Someone asked Salman "What is your ancestry?" so in reply to them Salman al Farsi said:

"My nobility lies in my religion, and my ancestry is soil. I was created from soil and I will return to soil. I will then be resurrected and proceed

towards the scales. If my scales are weighty, my ancestry will indeed be very noble. And how honorable I will be in the sight of my Allah who will admit me into Paradise! But if my scales are light, my ancestry will definitely be very ignoble. And how despicable I will be in the sight of my Allah who will punish me – unless He showers forgiveness and mercy over my sins."

Tariq ibn Shihab narrated that he spent a night with Salman Farsi to see what worship he engages in. Tariq said, "He got up and began performing prayer in the latter part of the night." Tariq expected more from him so he mentioned this to him and thereupon Salman replied:

"Safeguard the five daily prayers because they atone for sins provided they are not major sins. When people complete the isha prayer they depart in three ways:

1. The one who has a record against him and nothing in his favor.
2. The one who has a record in his favor and nothing against him.
3. The one who has no record in his favor and nothing against him.

The first one makes use of the darkness of the night and the obliviousness of people to get engrossed in sin. He has a record against him and nothing in his favor.

The second one makes use of the darkness of the night and the obliviousness of people to stand up in prayer. He has a record in his favor and nothing against him.

The third one performed prayer and went to sleep. He has no record in his favor and nothing against him.

Beware of overburdening yourself. Impose moderation and continuity [in your worship].

Salman al Farsi said:

"When Allah wills bad or destruction for a person, He removes modesty from him. You will therefore find him to be detestable and despicable.

When he is detestable and despicable, mercy is removed from him. And so, you will find him to be stern and hard-hearted. When this happens, trustworthiness is removed from him. This will result in his becoming treacherous and deceitful. When this happens the rope of Islam is removed from his neck. This will result in his becoming accursed and doomed."

Salman al Farsi said:

"The similitude of the heart and body is like a person who is paralyzed and one who is blind. The paralyzed man says: 'I see a date but I cannot stand up to get it, so carry me up.' The blind man carries him, he eats the date and also feeds it to the blind man."

Salman al Farsi said:

"Three things caused me to laugh and three things caused me to cry.

I laughed at:

1. *A person who has hopes in this world while death is pursuing him.*
2. *A person who is heedless, whereas Allah is fully aware of him.*
3. *A person who laughs with his mouth wide open, but does not know whether Allah is angry with him or pleased with him.*

I cried over:

1. *The separation from my beloveds - Muhammad and his companions.*
2. *The terrifying scene at the time when I will have to experience the pangs of death.*
3. *When I will stand before Allah not knowing whether I will be going towards the Hellfire or towards paradise."*

Salman al Farsi said:

"Every person has an external and an internal. When a person rectifies his external, Allah rectifies his internal. When a person corrupts his external, Allah corrupts his internal."

Salman al Farsi said:

"When you commit an evil in privacy, follow it with a good deed in privacy. When you commit an evil in public, follow it with a good deed in public. In this way the latter will be an atonement for the former."

Salman al Farsi said:

"The similitude of a believer in this world is like a sick man who has his doctor with him. The doctor knows his illness and the medicine which will treat him. When he desires something which will be harmful to him, the doctor refuses to give it to him, and says: 'Do not even go near it because if you consume it, it will destroy you.' The doctor continues prohibiting him until he is fully cured from his ailment.

Similar is the case of the believer – he desires many thing which others have been blessed with. But Allah does not give them to him and keeps him away from them until He takes his life away and admits him into Paradise."

Salman al Farsi said:

"A man entered Paradise on account of a fly, another entered Hell because of a fly."

People asked Salman: "How did that happen?"

Salman replied: *"Two men from one of the past nations came across some people with their idol. Whenever anyone came to them, he had to make an offering to the idol.*

The people said to one of them: 'Make an offering.'

He replied: 'I do not have anything.'

They said: 'Give anything, even if it is a fly.'

So he gave a fly as an offering, and continued on his way. He entered Hell because of this.

They said to another man: 'Make an offering.'

He replied: "I cannot make an offering to anyone apart from Allah."

So they killed him, and he entered Paradise."

A man once came to Salman and told him: *"Advise me."*

Salman said: *"Do not speak."*

The man said: *"A person who is living among people cannot abstain from speaking."*

Salman said: *"If you have to speak, speak what is right or remain silent."*

The man said: *"Give me more advice."*

Salman said: *"Do not become angry."*

The man said: *"I am overcome and unable to control myself."*

Salman said: *"When you become angry, restrain your tongue and hand."*

The man said: *"Give me more advice."*

Salman said: *"Do not intermingle with people."*

The man said: *"It is not possible for a person who lives among people not to intermingle with them."*

Salman said: *"If you have to intermingle with them, speak the truth and fulfill your trusts."*

Salman al Farsi said:

"A time will soon come when knowledge will be in the open but practicing on it will be hidden; people will maintain mutual contact verbally but their hearts will be cut off from each other. When they do this Allah will set a seal on their hearts, ears and eyes."

Salman al Farsi said:

"Adhere to moderation and continuity in your deeds, and you will be the horse which wins."

Salman al Farsi said:

"A person used to supplicate to Allah during times of prosperity. He is then afflicted by adversity. Now when he supplicates the angels say: 'We recognize this voice which is now coming from a weak man.' They intercede in his favor.

If a person was not in the habit of supplicating to Allah during times of prosperity and now supplicates when he is afflicted by adversity the angels say: 'We do not recognize this voice which is coming from a weak man.' They do not intercede in his favor."

Salman al Farsi wrote to Abu ad-Darda:

"You will never acquire what you want unless you cast aside what you desire. You will never acquire what you hope for unless you exercise patience over what you dislike.

Your speech should therefore be the remembrance of Allah, your silence must be for reflection, and your looking must be for admonishment. This world is constantly shifting and its splendour is changing, so do not be deceived by it. Make the masjid your house. Peace be to you."

Salman al Farsi said:

"If you befriend a wealthy person, beware of asking him anything if you want to maintain your position with him. This is because begging is a blight on the face of the beggar. The giver is forced to think highly of the person who returns what is given to him."

Salman al Farsi said:

"The person who engages in excessive optional acts while leaving out the obligatory ones is like a trader who loses his capital while he is seeking profits."

Salman al Farsi was once asked "What do you dislike about leadership?" so he replied:

"It is very sweet when one is breastfed with it, but very bitter when one is weaned off it."

Salman al Farsi said:

"What will you do in the following three situations:

1. *When a scholar errs.*
2. *When a hypocrite disputes through the Quran.*
3. *When the world chops off your necks [when you are reduced to poverty].*

As for the scholar, do not hand over matters of your religion to him.

As for the hypocrite who disputes through the Quran, you should know that the Quran has a light like the light of the road. So accept from him what you recognize as being from the Quran, and what you do not recognize, leave it to Allah.

As for the world chopping off your necks, look at those who are in a worse off condition than you, and do not look at those who are in a better condition than you."

Salman al Farsi wrote to Abu ad-Darda:

"Knowledge is like springs which people crowd, and this person and that person and many others are filled with it. Thus Allah enables many people to benefit from it. Words of wisdom which are not uttered are like a body without a soul. Knowledge which does not emanate is like a treasure which is not spent.

The similitude of a scholar is like a man who holds a lamp on a dark road. All those who pass by obtain light from it, and each of them supplicates in his favor."

Salman al Farsi said:

"I would rather die and be resurrected, die and be resurrected and again die and be resurrected than to see the private part of a Muslim or for a Muslim to see mine."

Salman al Farsi said:

"*People will continue experiencing goodness as long as the first generation teaches the next. But if the first departs before the next can learn, they will be destroyed.*"

Buqayrah, the wife of Salman, reported:

"*When Salman was on his deathbed, he called for me to his upper story room that had four doors. He said, 'O Buqayrah! Open all the doors because I shall have a few visitors today and I know not from which of these doors they will enter. He then asked for some musk and said, 'Dilute it in small container.' When I did this, he said, ' Sprinkle it all around my bed and then go and wait downstairs. When you come to look soon, you shall see something on my bed.' When I came to see, I saw him lying on his bed with his soul having already departed. He appeared as if he was sleeping.*"

A report by Ataa bin Saa'ib states Salman told his wife on his deathbed regarding the musk, "*Because tonight some angels will be coming to me who can smell fragrances but do not eat food.*"

The aforementioned Abdullah bin Salam reported that, "*Salman passed away and I was lying on my bed one afternoon when I happened to fall asleep. Salman then appeared in my dream and greeted me saying, 'As salaamu alyka wa rahmatullaha.' I responded by saying, 'As salaamu alyka wa rahmatullaha, O abu abdullah. How have you found your destination?' He replied, 'It is excellent. Hold fast to Tawakkul because Tawakkul is a most excellent virtue! Hold fast to Tawakkul because Tawakkul is a most excellent virtue!*"

Adi bin Hatim

Adi ibn Hatim was a Christian of the Ruqui sect of Christians. His father Hatim was chief of the Tayy tribe of the Najd province in central Arabia. After Hatim's death, his son Adi became the tribal leader and ruler. Adi was on the throne while he witnessed the Prophet winning continuous victories, while his influence and power and the scope of Islam began to expand. So Adi had foreseen that in a few days, they too would have no choice but to bow their heads in front of Allah's Messenger, so like other rulers, his arrogance was not satisfied with the subordination and rule of a minor Qureshi. However, stopping the rising flood of Islam was beyond their control, yet still the pride of the ruler did not allow them to bow down to Islam as a convert or tributary. Therefore, Adi decided his tribe should leave their homeland. They prepared their luggage, and started waiting for the arrival of the Islamic armies, and eventual migration to the Christian community of Syria. Adi told a boy from his subjects, "Bring me the fastest camel you have. If you hear an army of Muhammad is near our border inform me immediately." One day the boy came and said, "O my king, an army is approaching, and I have been told it is the army of Muhammad." Adi said, "Then bring the camel I asked you for, and gather my family. I will flee to Syria to live under the Christians because they follow my religion."

During the hasty withdrawal Adi's sister got left behind and the caravan was unable to go back to retrieve her so she was taken as a prisoner of war by the Muslim army during the invasion of the village of Adi. The captives were treated kindly and placed near the masjid so they could hear the call to prayer and witness the prayer. One day the Prophet Muhammad pbuh passed by the sister of Adi and she stood saying, "My father is dead, and my guardian is missing, set me free, may Allah be gracious to you." The Prophet said, "Who is your guardian?" she said, "Adi bin Hatim." The prophet said, "Adi, the one who fled from Allah and His Messenger?" then he walked away. The next day she said the same as she had said before, and the Prophet gave her the same response. The third day he walked past her and she did not say anything. A man behind the Prophet then motioned her to stand up and repeat her request. Thereupon she stood and said, "My father is dead and my guardian is missing, set me free, may Allah be gracious to you." The Prophet said, "I agree. But do not leave in haste until you find someone trustworthy to take you to your brother." Upon inquiring, she learned the man who was behind the Prophet that suggested she ask again was his son-in-law; Ali bin Abi Talib.

After finding some people from her tribe to accompany her, the Prophet gave Adi's sister clothes, food, wealth and a camel to ride and she traveled from Medinah, Arabia to Syria. Upon meeting Adi, his sister scolded him for leaving her alone behind out of all their family so she had to rely upon the kindness of others to survive. After some days had passed Adi asked her, "You are smart and wise, what opinion do you have about this person (the Prophet)?" She said, "I have this opinion. I think by Allah, that you should join him quickly. If he is a prophet, the one who hastens toward him would enjoy his grace. And if he is a king, you would not be disgraced in his sight while you are as you are." Adi appreciated and accepted this reasonable advice.

Adi described his meeting with the Prophet as follows:

"I went up to him while he was in the masjid. I greeted him and he said, 'Who is this man?' I said, 'I am Adi ibn Hatim.' He stood up for me, took me by the hand, and set off toward his house. By Allah, as he was walking with me toward his house, a weak old woman met him with her young child. She stopped him and began talking to him about a problem. As he was attending to her needs, I said to myself, 'By Allah this is not the behavior of a King.' He then took me by the hand and went with me until we reached his home. There he got a leather cushion filled with palm fiber, gave it to me, and said, 'Sit on this.' I felt embarrassed and said, 'Rather you sit on it.' He said, 'No, this is for you to sit on.' I deferred and sat on it, and he sat on the floor because he did not have another cushion. I said to myself, 'This is not the behavior of a king, and this is not the home of a king.' The Prophet said to me, 'O Adi, accept Islam and you will be safe!' I replied, 'I already have a religion.' The prophet said, 'I know more about

your religion than you do. Are you not from the Rukusiyyah; a sect between Christianity and Sabeans? And when you go to war, you take one quarter of your people's spoils? And is this not prohibited in your religion?' I said, 'Indeed this is correct.' At this moment, I knew he was a Prophet sent by Allah, because he was knowledgeable of affairs we were ignorant of.

The Prophet said, 'I know what is preventing you from accepting Islam. You think the only people to follow this religion are the oppressed people who have no strength. O Adi, have you heard of al-Hira(a city in Iraq)?' I said, 'I have not seen it, but I have heard of it.' The Prophet said, 'I swear by the One Who has my soul in His Hand, Allah will complete this affair until a woman travels from al-Hira to make circumambulation around the Kabah without fearing anyone.' The Prophet said, 'O Adi, perhaps what prevents you from entering Islam is the poverty of the Muslims. I swear by the One Who has my soul in His Hand the treasures of Khosrow bin Hormuz will be seized.' I said, 'The treasures of Khosrow bin Hormuz?'(the then ruler of the superpower Persia) The Prophet said, 'Yes, Khosrow, and money will be so abundant until people would refuse to accept it.'

After hearing that, Adi bin Hatim embraced Islam. Adi lived a long life until the age of 120 years old fighting in many battles, even losing his eye in the battle of Jamal. Adi died in Kufa in 67 AH.

Adi bin Hatim said, "*Indeed, I have lived to see two affairs mentioned by the Prophet come to pass, and the third will surely come to pass as well. I was part of the calvary that descended upon the treasures of Khosrow and seized them. And I have seen the women leaving al-Hira on her camel, fearing nothing until she arrived at the Sacred House.*"

Allah fulfilled the third prophecy of the Messenger of Allah during the Caliphate of Umar ibn Abdul Aziz. Wealth became so abundant during his reign that when zakat charity was collected there was nobody found to be in need for it to be distributed to.

The Prophet used to deal with each new Muslim according to his rank and the rank of those who were before Islam was maintained after entering Islam. Adi was the ruler of the Tayy Tribe, so after his conversion to Islam the Prophet gifted him with the ruling of the Tayy Tribe.

Narrated `Adi bin Hatim heard the Prophet (ﷺ) saying:

"Save yourself from Hell-fire even by giving half a date-fruit in charity."

Source: Sahih al-Bukhari 1417

Narrated `Adi bin Hatim:

Allah's Messenger said, "There will be none among you but his Lord will speak to him, and there will be no interpreter between them nor a screen to screen Him."

Source: Sahih al-Bukhari 7443

It was narrated from 'Adi bin Hatim that :

the Messenger of Allah, said: "Whoever swears an oath then sees that something else is better than it, let him do that which is better and offer expiation for what he swore about. "

Source: Sunan Ibn Majah 2108 Grade: Sahih

It was narrated that 'Adi bin Hatim said:

"I said: 'O Messenger of Allah, what if I shoot the game but it vanishes at night?' He said: 'If you find your arrow in it and you do not find anything else, then eat it.'"

Source: Sunan Ibn Majah 3213 Grade: Sahih

Narrated `Adi bin Hatim:

I said, "O Allah's Messenger! What is the meaning of the white thread distinct from the black thread? Are these two threads?" He said, "You are not intelligent if you watch the two threads." He then added, "No, it is the darkness of the night and the whiteness of the day.''

Source: Sahih al-Bukhari 4510

Narrated 'Adi bin Hatim:

I asked the Prophet about game killed by Mir'ad. So he said: 'What you kill by its sharp edge then eat it, and what you kill by its broad side then, it was killed by something blunt.'"

Source: Jami` at-Tirmidhi 1471 Grade: Sahih

Narrated Adi ibn Hatim:

I said: Messenger of Allah, tell me when one of us catches game and has no knife; may he slaughter with a flint and a splinter of stick. He said: Cause the blood to flow with whatever you like and mention Allah's name.

Source: Sunan Abi Dawud 2824 Grade: Sahih

Sha'bi said:

"When 'Adi bin Hatim came to Kufah, we came to him with a delegation of the Fuqaha of Kufah and said to him: 'Tell us of something that you heard from the Messenger of Allah.' He said: 'I came to the Prophet and he said: "O 'Adi bin Hatim, enter Islam and you will be safe." I said, "What is Islam?" He said: "To testify to La ilaha illallah (none has the right to be worshipped but Allah) and that I am the Messenger of Allah, and to believe in all the Divine Decrees, the good of them and the bad of them, the sweet of them and the bitter of them."

Source: Sunan Ibn Majah 87 Grade: Daif

Narrated `Adi bin Hatim:

I asked the Prophet (about the hunting dogs) and he replied, "If you let loose (with Allah's name) your tamed dog after a game and it hunts it, you may eat it, but if the dog eats of (that game) then do not eat it because the dog has hunted it for itself." I further said, "Sometimes I send my dog for hunting and find another dog with it. He said, "Do not eat the game for you have mentioned Allah's name only on sending your dog and not the other dog."

Source: Sahih al-Bukhari 175

Narrated `Adi bin Hatim:

The Prophet said, "There will be none among you but will be talked to by Allah on the Day of Resurrection, without there being an interpreter between him and Him (Allah). He will look and see nothing ahead of him, and then he will look (again for the second time) in front of him, and the (Hell) Fire will confront him. So, whoever among you can save himself from the Fire, should do so even with one half of a date (to give in charity).

Source: Sahih al-Bukhari 6539

Narrated `Adi bin Hatim:

The Prophet said, "Protect yourself from the Fire." He then turned his face aside (as if he were looking at it) and said again, "Protect yourself from the Fire," and then turned his face aside (as if he were looking at it), and he said so for the third time till we thought he was looking at it. He then said, "Protect yourselves from the Fire, even if with one half of a date and he who hasn't got even this, (should do so) by (saying) a good, pleasant word.'

Source: Sahih al-Bukhari 6540

Narrated 'Adi bin Hatim:

"I came to the Prophet while I had a cross of gold around my neck. He said: 'O 'Adi! Remove this idol from yourself!' And I heard him reciting from Surah Bara'ah: They took their rabbis and monks as lords besides Allah (9:31). He said: 'As for them, they did not worship them, but when they made something lawful for them, they considered it lawful, and when they made something unlawful for them, they considered it unlawful.'"

Source: Jami` at-Tirmidhi 3095 Grade: Daif

Narrated `Adi bin Hatim:

We came to `Umar in a delegation (during his rule). He started calling the men one by one, calling each by his name. (As he did not call me early) I said to him. "Don't you know me, O chief of the Believers?" He said, "Yes, you embraced Islam when they (i.e. your people) disbelieved; you have come (to the Truth) when they ran away; you fulfilled your promises when they broke theirs; and you recognized it (i.e. the Truth of Islam) when they denied it." On that, `Adi said, "I therefore don't care."

Source: Sahih al-Bukhari 4394

Narrated 'Adi bin Hatim At-Tai:

That he asked the Messenger of Allah, "Which charity is most virtuous?" He said, "The service of a worshipper in the cause of Allah, or providing the shade of tent, or mount in the cause of Allah."

Source: Jami` at-Tirmidhi 1626 Grade: Hasan

Narrated `Adi bin Hatim:

While I was sitting with Allah's Messenger (p.b.u.h) two person came to him; one of them complained about his poverty and the other complained about the prevalence of robberies. Allah's Messenger said, "As regards stealing and robberies, there will shortly come a time when a caravan will go to Mecca (from Medina) without any guard. And regarding poverty, The Hour (Day of Judgment) will not be established till one of you wanders about with his object of charity and will not find anybody to accept it And (no doubt) each one of you will stand in front of Allah and there will be neither a curtain nor an interpreter between him and Allah, and Allah will ask him, 'Did not I give you wealth?' He will reply in the affirmative. Allah will further ask, 'Didn't I send a messenger to you?' And again that person will reply in the affirmative Then he will look to his right and he will see nothing but Hell-fire, and then he will look to his left and will see nothing but Hell-fire. And so, any (each one) of you should save himself from the fire even by giving half of a date-fruit (in charity).

And if you do not find a half datefruit, then (you can do it through saying) a good pleasant word (to your brethren).

Source: Sahih al-Bukhari 1413

Umar ibn 'Abdu'l-'Aziz asked Abu Bakr ibn Abi Hathama, "Why did Abu Bakr write, 'From Abu Bakr, the Khalifa (Successor) of the Messenger of Allah' and then 'Umar wrote after him, 'From 'Umar ibn al-Khattab, the khalifa (successor) of Abu Bakr'? Who was the first to write 'the Amir al-Mu'minin'?" He replied, "My grandmother, ash-Shifa', related to me, and she was one of the first to write 'the Amir al-Mu'minin'?" He said, "My grandfather, ash-Shifa' related to me, (and she was one of the first Muhajirun and when 'Umar ibn al-Khattab entered the market, he visited her), saying, "Umar ibn al-Khattab wrote to the governor of Iraq requesting him to send him two trustworthy noble men so that he could question them about Iraq and its people. He sent him a master of Iraq, Labid ibn Rabi'a and also 'Adi ibn Hatim, and they came to Madina. They made their camels kneel in the courtyard of the mosque, entered it and found 'Amr ibn al-'As. They said to him, "Amr, ask permission for us to visit the Amir al-Mu'minin, 'Umar.' 'Amr got up and went to 'Umar. He said, 'Peace be upon you, Amir al-Mu'minin.' 'Umar said to him, 'Ibn al-'As, what made you use this name? You have deviated from what you normally say.' He said, 'Yes, Labid ibn Rabi'a and <u>'Adi ibn Hatim came and said to me, "Ask permission for us to visit the Amir al-Mu'minin."</u> I said, "You two, by Allah, have hit upon the correct name. He is the amir and we are the believers.'" The title originated on that day."

Source: Al-Adab Al-Mufrad 1023 Grade: Sahih

Adi bin Hatim said:

"I went to the Prophet while he was sitting in the Masjid, the people said: 'This is 'Adi bin Hatim.' And I came without having a treaty nor a writ. When I was brought to him, he took my hand. Prior to that he had said: 'I

hope that Allah will place his hand in my hand.'" He said: "He stood with me, and a woman and a boy met him and said: 'We have a need from you.' He stood with them, until he was finished dealing with what they wanted. Then he took me by the hand until he brought me to his house. A slave girl brought him a cushion to sit on, and I sat in front of him. He expressed thanks and praise for Allah then said: 'What has caused you to flee from saying La Ilaha Illallah? Do you know of another god other than Him?'" He said: "I said: 'No.'" He said: "Then he talked for some time, and then said: 'You refuse to say Allahu Akbar because you know that there is something greater than Allah?'" He said: "I said: 'No.' He said: 'Indeed the Jews are those who Allah is wrath with, and the Christians have strayed.'" He said: "I said: 'Indeed I am a Muslim, Hanif.'" He said: "I saw his face smiling with happiness." He said: "Then he ordered that I stop with him at the home of a man from the Ansar, whom he would frequently visit in the mornings and the evenings. When I was with him at night, a people in woolen garments of these Nimar (a cloth with certain patters, and the word appeared before) came. Then he performed Salat and stood to encourage them (the people) to give (charity) to them. Then he said: 'Even with a Sa' or half a Sa', or a handful or part of a handful, to save the face of one of you from the heat of Hell, or the Fire. And even if it be by a date or a part of a date - for indeed one of you shall meet Allah and it shall be said to him what I say to you: "Have I not given hearing and seeing to you?" He shall say: "Of course." It will be said: "Have I not given you wealth and children?" He shall say: "Of course." It will be said: "So where is what you have sent forth for yourself?" He will look before him and behind him, on his right and on his left, but he shall not find anything to protect his face from the heat of Hell. Let one of you protect his face from the Fire, even if with part of a date, and if he does not find that, then with a good statement. For indeed I do not fear poverty for you - Allah will aid you and grant you, such that a woman can travel on her camel howda from Yathrib to Al-Hirah, or further, without fear of being robbed.' I began thinking to myself: "Where would the thieves of Taiy' be then?"'

Source: Jami` at-Tirmidhi 2953b Grade: Hasan

Adi bin Hatim said:

"You will remain in a good state as long as you do not approve what you used to know to be wrong or censure what you used to know to be right, and as long as the knowledgeable (scholar) amongst you can speak amongst you without fear."

Tamim ibn Aws al Dari

Tamim al Dari was a Christian from the tribe of Laham. His full name and lineage was Tamim bin Aus bin Harja Ibne Soor bin Hazeem bin Zarai bin Adi bin Aldar bin Hani bin Habib bin Tamara bin Laham bin Adi bin Umar bin Sabaa. He lived in Syria before moving to Arabia to embrace Islam. Tamim would lead the Taraweeh prayer during the Khilafah of Umar.

Tamim related his story as follows:

"I was in Syria when the messenger of Allah was sent as a Prophet. I went out to take care of some work once when night caught up with me. As was the superstitious custom, I said, 'Tonight I am in the protection of the master (jinn) of this valley.' When I lay down to sleep, I heard someone whom I could not see. He was calling out, 'Seek protection from Allah because the Jinn cannot protect anyone against Allah!' I exclaimed, 'By Allah! What are you saying?' the voice said, 'The prophet of the unlettered people has made his appearance. He is the Messenger of Allah and we performed prayer behind him in Hajoon, where we accepted Islam and followed him. The ploys of the jinn (to eavesdrop on the conversations of the angels and convey the news of future events to fortune-tellers) is over and they are now being pelted by flaming stars. You had better go to Muhammad who is the prophet of the Lord of the Universe.'

I then went to the town of Dayr Ayoob in Palestine, where I consulted a monk and related the incident to him. The monk said "They (the Jinn) have told you the truth. He (Muhammad) will make his appearance in the sacred land (Mecca) and the place to which he will migrate will also be a sacred land (Medinah). He is the best of all prophets and do not allow anyone to beat you to him." I then mustered up all the courage I had, went to the Messenger of Allah and embraced Islam."

Fatimah, daughter of Qais, said:

I heard the crier of the Messenger of Allah calling: Assemble for the prayer. I Then came out and prayed along with the Messenger of Allah : When the Messenger of Allah finished his prayer, he sat on the pulpit laughing, and he said : Everyone should remain where he had said his prayer. He then asked : Do you know why I have assembled you? They said: Allah and His Messenger know best. He said: I did not call you together for some alarming news or for something good. Rather, I called you all because Tamim al-Dari, a Christian, who came and accepted Islam, told me something which agrees with what I was telling you about the Dajjal(Antichrist). He told me that he sailed with thirty men of Lakhm and Judham and that they were storm-tossed for a month. They drew near to an island when the sun was setting. They sat in a boat nearest to them and entered the island where they were met by a very hairy beast. They said: Woe to you! What can you be ? It replied : I am the Jassasah. Go to this man in the monastery, for he is anxious to get news of you. He said : When it named a man to us we were afraid of it lest it should be a she-devil. So we went off quickly and entered the monastery, where we found a man with the hugest and strongest frame we had ever seen with his hands chained to his neck. He then narrated the rest of the tradition. He asked them about the palm-trees of Baisan and the spring of Zughar and about the unlettered prophet. He said: I am the false-messiah (the Antichrist) and will be soon given permission to emerge. And the Prophet said: He is in the Syrian sea or the Yemeni sea: No, on the contrary, it is towards the east that he is. He said it twice and pointed his hand to the east. She said: I memorized this (tradition) from the Messenger of Allah, and she narrated the tradition.

Source: Sunan Abi Dawud 4326 Grade: Sahih

Amir b. Sharahil Sha'bi Sha'b Hamdan reported that he asked Fatima, daughter of Qais and sister of ad-Dahhak b. Qais and she was the first amongst the emigrant women:

Narrate to me a hadith which you had heard directly from Allah's Messenger and there is no extra link in between them. She said: Very well, if you like, I am prepared to do that, and he said to her: Well, do It and narrate that to me. She said: I married the son of Mughira and he was a chosen young man of Quraish at that time, but he fell as a martyr in the first Jihad (fighting) on the side of Allah's Messenger. When I became a widow, 'Abd al-Rahman b. Auf, one amongst the group of the Companions of Allah's Messenger, sent me the proposal of marriage. Allah's Messenger also sent me such a message for his freed slave Usama b. Zaid. And it had been conveyed to me that Allah's Messenger had said (about Usama): He who loves me should also love Usama. When Allah's Messenger talked to me (about this matter), I said: My affairs are in your hand. You may marry me to anyone whom you like. He said: You better shift now to the house of Umm Sharik, and Umm Sharik was a rich lady from amongst the Ansar. She spent generously for the cause of Allah and entertained guests very hospitably. I said: Well, I will do as you like. He said: Do not do that for Umm Sharik is a woman who is very frequently visited by guests and I do not like that your head may be uncovered or the cloth may be removed from your shank and the strangers may catch sight of them which you abhor. You better shift to the house of your cousin 'Abdullah b. 'Amr b. Umm Maktum and he is a person of the Bani Fihr branch of the Quraish, and he belonged to that tribe (to which Fatima) belonged. So I shifted to that house, and when my period of waiting was over, I heard the voice of an announcer making an announcement that the prayer would be observed in the mosque (where) congregational prayer (is observed). So I set out towards that mosque and observed prayer along with Allah's Messenger and I was in the row of the women which was near the row of men. When Allah's Messenger had finished his prayer, he sat on the pulpit smiling and said: Every worshipper should keep sitting at his place. He then said: Do you know why I had asked you to assemble? They said: Allah and His Messenger know best. He said: By Allah. I have not made you assemble for exhortation or for a warning, but I have detained you here, for Tamim Dari, a Christian, who came and accepted Islam, told me something, which agrees with what I was telling, you about the Dajjal(Antichrist). He narrated to me that he had sailed in a ship along with thirty men of Bani Lakhm and Bani Judham and had been tossed by waves in the ocean for a month. Then these (waves) took them (near) the land within the ocean (island) at the time of sunset. They sat in a small side-boat and entered that island. There was a beast with long thick hair (and because of these) they could not distinguish his face from his back. They said: Woe to you, who can you be? Thereupon it said: I am al-Jassasa. They said: What is al-Jassasa? And it said: O people, go to this person in the monastery as he is very much eager to know about you. He (the narrator) said: When it named a person for us we were afraid of it lest it should be a devil. Then we hurriedly went on till we came to that monastery and found a well-built person there with his hands tied to his neck and having iron shackles between his two legs up to the ankles. We said: Woe be upon thee, who are you? And he said: You would soon come to know about me. but tell me who are you. We said: We are people from Arabia and we embarked upon a boat but the sea-waves had been driving us for one month and they brought as near this island. We got into the side-boats and entered this island and here a beast met us with profusely thick hair and because of the thickness of his hair his face could not be distinguished from his back. We said: Woe be to thee, who are you? It said: I am al- Jassasa. We said: What is al-Jassasa? And it said: You go to this very person in the monastery for he is eagerly waiting for you to know about you. So we came to you in hot haste fearing that that might be the Devil. He (that chained person) said: Tell me about the date-palm trees of Baisan. We said: About what aspect of theirs do you seek information? He said: I ask you whether these trees bear fruit or not. We said: yes. Thereupon he said: I think these would not bear fruits. He said: Inform me about the lake of Tabariyya? We said: Which aspect of it do you want to know? He said: Is there water in it? They said: There is abundance of water in it. Thereupon he said: I think it would soon become dry. He again said: Inform me about the spring of Zughar. They said: Which aspect of it you want to know? He (the chained person) said: Is there water in it and does it irrigate (the land)? We said to him: Yes, there is abundance of water in it and the inhabitants (of Medina) irrigate (land) with the help of it, He said: Inform me about the unlettered Prophet; what has he done? We said: He has come out from Mecca and has settled In Yathrib (Medina). He said: Do the Arabs fight against him? We said: Yes. He said: How did he deal with them? We informed him that he had overcome those in his neighborhood and they had submitted themselves before him. Thereupon he said to us: Has it actually happened? We said: Yes. Thereupon he said: If it is so that is better for them that they should show obedience to him. I am going to tell you about myself and I am Dajjal(Anti-christ) and would be soon permitted to get out and so I shall get out and travel in the land, and will not spare any town where I would not stay for forty nights except Mecca and Medina as these two (places) are prohibited (areas) for me and I would not make an attempt to enter any one of these two. An angel with a sword in his hand would confront me and would bar my way and there would be angels to guard every passage leading to it; then Allah's Messenger striking the pulpit with the help of the end of his staff said: This implies Taiba meaning Medina. Have I not, told you an account (of the Dajjal) like this? 'The people said: Yes, and this account narrated by Tamim Dari was liked by me for it corroborates the account which I gave to you in regard to him (Dajjal) at Medina and Mecca. Behold he (Dajjal) is in the Syrian sea (Mediterranean) or the Yemen sea (Arabian sea). Nay, on the contrary, he is in the east, he is in the east, he is in the east, and he pointed with his hand towards the east. I (Fatima bint Qais) said: I preserved it in my mind (this narration from Allah's Messenger).

Source: Sahih Muslim 2942a

Narrated Tamim ad-Dari:

Tamim asked: Messenger of Allah, what is the sunnah about a man who accepts Islam by advice and persuasion of a Muslim? He replied: He is the nearest to him in life and in death.

Source: Sunan Abi Dawud 2918 Grade: Hasan Sahih

It is narrated on the authority of Tamim ad-Dari that the Prophet (ﷺ) said:

"The Religion is sincerity." We said, "To whom?" He said "To Allah, to His Book, To His Messenger, and to the leaders of the Muslims and their masses."

Source: Sahih Muslim 55a

It was narrated that Tamim Ad-Dari said:

"I heard the Messenger of Allah say: 'Whoever ties a horse in the cause of Allah, then feeds it with his own hand, he will have one merit for every grain.'"

Source: Sunan Ibn Majah 2791 Grade: Hasan

It was narrated from Tamim Dari that the Prophet (ﷺ) said:

"The first thing for which a person will be brought to account on the Day of Resurrection will be his prayer. If it is complete, then the voluntary (prayers) will also be recorded for him (as an increase). If it is not complete then Allah will say to His angels: 'Look and see whether you find any voluntary prayers for My slave, and take them to make up what is lacking from his obligatory prayers.' Then all his deeds will be reckoned in like manner."

Source: Sunan Ibn Majah 1426 Grade: Sahih

Tamim Ad-Dari narrated that:

The Messsenger of Allah said: "Whoever says ten times: 'I bear witness that none has the right to be worshipped but Allah. Alone, without partner, One Deity, the One, As-Samad, He did not take a wife, nor a child, nor is there anyone like Him, (Ash-hadu an lā ilāha illallāh, waḥdahu lā sharīka lahu, ilahan wahidan, aḥadan ṣamadan lam yattakhidh ṣāḥibatan wa lā waladan wa lam yakun lahu kufuwan aḥad)' Allah will write for him forty million good deeds."

Source: Jami` at-Tirmidhi 3473 Grade: Daif

When Tamim came to Medina from Syria, he brought some lanterns and a kerosene oil with him. Upon reaching Medina, he put the oil into the lanterns and hung them in the Prophet's Mosque. In the evening, these lanterns were lit. Before this, there was no source of lighting in the mosque. When the Prophet came to the mosque and found the mosque lit, he inquired who arranged for the lighting. The companion named Tamim, the Prophet became so happy that he said if I had a daughter I would have given her in marriage to Tamim. Nofal bin Haris was present there and he made an offer of his widowed daughter Ume Al Mughira for marriage with Tamim. The Prophet then offered the marriage of Ume Al Mughira with Tamim during the same sitting. Tamim had 1 child, a daughter name Ruqayya. Tamim al Dari died in 40 AH.

Abraha the Ethiopian

Some historians narrate there were two different Abraha's of Ethiopian heritage that were Christian who both accepted Islam and met Muhammad pbuh. Other historians say there was only one. Yet with certainty there was at least one Ethiopian Christian named Abraha who became a Muslim Sahabi. It is believed he/they were in Ethiopia when Jafar and his fellow Muslim migrants presented Islam to the Negus whereupon Abraha accepted Islam before migrating to Medinah.

Idris

Idris was another Christian who embraced Islam in Ethiopia and migrated along with Jafar and Abraha back to Medinah to meet the Prophet Muhammad in person.

Usaid bin Saeed

After the Battle of Banu Qurayza, when the matter of the Jewish tribe of Banu Qurayza was handed over by the Messenger of Allah ﷺ to Sad bin Muaz, that whatever he decides will be acted upon accordingly, Saad bin Muaz decided that all men in the tribe be executed and the women and children be turned into slaves.

When news of this decision came to Usaid, he along with his friends went to Banu Qurayza and said, *"Don't you people remember the saying of Ibn Al Haiban What did you promise? O Jews, fear Allah and follow this truthful Prophet!"* Ibn Al Haiban was a Jewish scholar, who had migrated from Syria to Medina, there the Jews of Medina used to ask him to say prayers for them at the times of famine and other troubles. When Ibn al Haiban was on his deathbed he gathered the Jews and asked them if they knew why he left the lush green place like Syria and came to non-green place like Medina? *"I came here because I was waiting for a prophet who will migrate here. If I were alive, I would follow him. Look! You people should not avoid obeying him. Otherwise, this will mark your execution."* So the Jewish tribe of Banu Qurayza promised that they will do exactly as told and believe in the promised prophet when he migrates to them. But when Muhammad pbuh migrated to them as Ibn Al Haibain predicted the Jews avoided accepting Islam and obeying it and instead betrayed and combatted the Muslims. After witnessing the truth of the prediction Ibn al Haiban gave regarding the execution of Banu Qurayza after the Battle of Banu Qurayza, Usaid came with a few companions of his to the Prophet and accepted Islam and became a Muslim abandoning Judaism.

Asad ibn Saya al Qurathi

✝

Thalaba ibn Saya

✝

Asad ibn Ubaid

Asad ibn Saya, Thalaba and Asad ibn Ubaid were from the Jews who embraced Islam in Medinah. They all became Muslims because of their experience with ibn al-Haiban who predicted the promised prophet as foretold by the Taurat revealed to Moses who would migrate to Medinah. Their story is as follows:

"There was a Jewish man from Syria who we met two years before Islam in Medinah. By Allah, we never saw a man who did not pray the five daily prayers who was better than him. He stayed amongst us, and when the drought came, we went to him and said, 'O ibn al-Haiban, pray for rain on our behalf.' He replied, 'No by Allah, not until you pay your zakat which is due.' We said, 'How much is due?' He replied, 'A sa of dates of two mudd of barley.' Thus we paid our zakat. Then he went out and prayed for rain. By Allah, we did not depart our gathering before the clouds began to pour rain. This happened more than once, twice, or three times. We were present when death approached him. When he was certain he was going to die, he said, 'O Jews, do you know why I left the land of bread and wine (Syria) and came to the land of misery and hunger? (Medinah)' We replied, 'You know better than we.' He said, 'I came here to await the arrival of a Prophet whose time has arrived. This is the town he will migrate to. I was hoping for him to appear so I can follow him. You have reached his arrival, so do not let anyone precede you to him. Surely, he will defeat those who oppose him, and take them as captives. So do not allow that to keep you away from him.' When the

Prophet arrived in Medinah, the Jewish tribe Banu Qurayza was present. These three men were youths at the time but despite their age openly declared: 'O Banu Qurayza, verily he is the prophet ibn al Haiban promised you would come.' The Jews said, 'It is not him.' The youth said, "We swear by Allah, this is him, just as he was described.' So these three went to the Prophet and embraced Islam.

Asad bin Ka'ab bin Qurayzi

His name was Asad and his father's name was Ka'ab bin Asad, he had was from the Jewish tribe of Banu Qurayza in Medinah. It is believed he became Muslim on the day of Qurayza. After he accepted Islam, Jews made him the target of ridicule and humiliation. Yet he patiently bore all these hardships and troubles with a smiling face. After his association with Islam, he never disassociated himself from it, even though his prior relationships were shattered he chose his faith over his family/friends.

Usaid bin Ka'ab Al Qurayzi

His name was Usaid and his father's name was Ka'ab bin Asad. He was the blood brother of the previously mentioned Asad bin Ka'ab and was likewise ostracized from his Jewish family and friends after his acceptance of Islam. It is believed that Usaid and Asad probably both became Muslim on the same day.

Ashraf Habishi

His name was Ashraf and he was a Christian who accepted Islam in Ethiopia along with the aforementioned Abraha and Idris. Then he migrated when Jafar migrated with the Muslims of Ethiopia to Medinah.

Bustani al-Israeli

Bustani al-Israeli was a Jew who asked the Messenger of Allah about the names of the stars Prophet Joseph saw in his dream. Al-Baghawi reported in his commentary on the Quran that: *"The Prophet said, 'If I inform you, will you accept Islam?' He said, 'Yes.' Thus he informed him, and he embraced Islam."*

Bashir ibn Muawiyah

Bashir was a Christian and the brother of the Christian bishop Asqaf Najran. Bashir and his brother were deputed by the people of Najran to investigate Muhammad when his invitation to Islam came to them. After meeting with the prophet they were given a letter to take back to their people in Najran. The leader of the delegation read the letter out loud while they were traveling back, and while the letter was read the donkey of Bashir stumbled. In response to his donkey stumbling Bashir disparaged the Messenger of Allah. After Bashir did this his brother Asqaf scolded him and said, "You are speaking about a prophet who was sent." So Bashir replied, "By Allah, it is no offense. I will not exonerate him until I meet him." So with haste Bashir turned his donkey around and headed back to Medinah and embraced Islam. After embracing Islam he spent the remainder of his life with the prophet and is believed to have attained martyrdom during one of the battles. He was also known as Abu Alqama.

The meeting of the delegation of Najran and the contents of the first invitation to Islam and the contents of the letter Bashir and his brother were taking back to the people of Najran are related by the grandfather of Abd Yasoo, who was also a Christian before accepting Islam. After mentioning his chain of transmission Abd Yasoo said the first letter was sent before Surah Naml was revealed therefore it didn't start with "Bismillahir Rahmaanir Raheem". The first invitation letter said:

"I begin in the name of the God of Abraham, Isaac and Jacob. From Muhammad the Prophet and Messenger of Allah. To the high priest and people of Najraan. Peace be upon you. Before you I praise the God of Abraham, Isaac and Jacob. I call you from the worship of Allah's slaves to the worship of Allah and from the friendship of Allah's slaves to the friendship of Allah. Should you refuse (to accept Islam), you shall have to pay the jizya and should you refuse even this, I shall have to declare war against you. "

When the high priest read the letter he was alarmed and frightened. He immediately sent for Shurahbeel bin Wadaa'ah from the Hamdan tribe. Whenever any problem arose he was summoned first before any heroes, leaders or elites. The high priest handed over the Prophet's letter to Shurahbeel who read it. The high priest asked, "What is your opinion?" Shurahbeel said, "You know well that Allah promised Abraham prophethood in the progeny of his son Ismail. It would come as no surprise if this is the very person. (who has received the promised prophethood) I can offer no opinion in the matter of prophethood. Had the matter been a worldly one, I would have advised you and exerted myself to assist you." The high priest bade Shurahbeel to be seated and he sat down to the side.

Next the high priest sent for Abdullah bin Shurahbeel who belonged to the Dhu Asbah branch of Himyar tribe. The high priest read the letter to him and received a similar reply so he asked Abdullah to step aside and sit, so he did.

Then the high priest sent for Jabbar bin Faydh who belonged to a branch of Banul Himaas tribe. When the high priest read the letter to him again a similar reply was given so he asked Jabbar to sit as well, so he did.

Once they all agreed the high priest requested the bells to be rung, fires to be lit and flags waved in churches. This was the common practice whenever trouble occurred during the day. All the people in the valley gathered in response to the signal. In total there were 73 villages comprising 120,000 warriors.

When the high priest read the letter of the Messenger of Allah to them, everyone agreed that Shurahbeel bin Wadaa'ah from the Hamdan tribe, Abdullah bin Shurahbeel from the Dhu Asbah tribe and Jabbar bin Faydh and others should be sent to gather news from the Messenger of Allah directly. So the delegation left for Medinah.

Upon arrival they removed their traveling clothes and wore long decorative garments from Yemen which dragged on the ground along with golden rings. When they approached the Prophet and greeted him, the Prophet refused to reply to their greeting the entire day. So they looked for some people they knew from the Prophet's companions and found Uthman bin Affan and Abdur Rahman bin Awf. They told them: "O Uthman! O Abdur Rahman! Your Prophet wrote a letter to us and we have arrived in response to the letter. However, when we came to him and greeted him, he did not reply to our greeting and although we searched all day for an opportunity to speak to him, we have been unable to do so. What is your opinion? Do you think that we should return?"

The prophet's son-in-law Ali bin Abi Talib was also present so Uthman and Abdur Rahman asked him, "What do you think of these people, O Abul Hasan?" Addressing Uthman and Abdur Rahman, Ali said, "I think they should remove these clothes and these rings and wear their traveling clothes. Thereafter they should return to the Messenger of Allah."

When they did this and again greeted the Messenger of Allah, he replied to their greeting and said, "I swear by the Being Who has sent me with the truth that the Devil was certainly with you when you came to me the first time." The Messenger of Allah then asked about them and they asked him questions. During the course of their questioning they asked, "What have you to say about Jesus? We are Christians and will be returning to our people. If you are a Prophet, we would be pleased to hear what you have to say about him." The Messenger of Allah said to them, "I have nothing much to say about him today. Stay a while longer until I am able to inform you what my Lord has to say about Jesus."

By the following morning, the following verses of the Quran had been revealed:

إِنَّ مَثَلَ عِيسَىٰ عِندَ ٱللَّهِ كَمَثَلِ ءَادَمَ خَلَقَهُۥ مِن تُرَابٍ ثُمَّ قَالَ لَهُۥ كُن فَيَكُونُ (٥٩) ٱلْحَقُّ مِن رَّبِّكَ فَلَا تَكُن مِّنَ ٱلْمُمْتَرِينَ (٦٠) فَمَنْ حَآجَّكَ فِيهِ مِنۢ بَعْدِ مَا جَآءَكَ مِنَ ٱلْعِلْمِ فَقُلْ تَعَالَوْاْ نَدْعُ أَبْنَآءَنَا وَأَبْنَآءَكُمْ وَنِسَآءَنَا وَنِسَآءَكُمْ وَأَنفُسَنَا وَأَنفُسَكُمْ ثُمَّ نَبْتَهِلْ فَنَجْعَل لَّعْنَتَ ٱللَّهِ عَلَى ٱلْكَٰذِبِينَ (٦١)

Verily, the likeness of 'Īsā (Jesus) before Allâh is the likeness of Adam. He created him from dust, then (He) said to him: "Be!" - and he was. (59) (This is) the truth from your Lord, so be not of those who doubt. (60) Then whoever disputes with you concerning him ['Īsā (Jesus)] after (all this) knowledge that has come to you, [i.e. 'Īsā (Jesus)] being a slave of Allâh, and having no share in Divinity) say: (O Muhammad) "Come, let us call our sons and your sons, our women and your women, ourselves and yourselves - then we pray and invoke (sincerely) the Curse of Allâh upon those who lie." (61)

After the Prophet recited these verses to them, they refused to accept the challenge to invoke curses on the liars amongst the two opposing parties. The next morning the Prophet arrived for the challenge together with his grandsons Hasan and Husain and his daughter Fatima and his wives. Upon seeing this Shurahbeel said, "You know well that the people from the entire top and bottom parts of our valley always return content with my decisions. I swear by Allah that what I see here is an extremely serious and weighty affair. If he is a sent Messenger, we shall be the first Arabs to be an eyesore for him and the first to oppose him. This insult will not leave his heart nor the hearts of his companions until they destroy us. We are also the closest Arabs to them (and are most prone to any pending attacks). If he is a sent Messenger of Allah, then to engage him in mutually invoking curses would even destroy the hairs and fingernails of each of us on earth."

The delegation asked Shurahbeel, "What then is your proposal?" Shurahbeel said, "I propose that we negotiate (a treaty) with him for I do not see him to be one who would ever make futile clauses." They said, "We leave you to do as you see appropriate."

Shurahbeel went to see the Messenger of Allah and said, "I propose something better than mutually invoking curses." The prophet asked, "What is that?" Shurahbeel replied, "You have today and tonight to pass judgement (formulate the clauses of a treaty). We are prepared to accept whatever clauses you make." The Messenger of Allah asked him, 'Perhaps there are people left behind who may criticize you (for this).' Shurahbeel referred him to ask the delegation. When the Prophet asked the delegation they said, "the people from the entire top and bottom parts of our valley always return content with the decisions of Shurahbeel." The Messenger of Allah then returned home without carrying out the mutual invoking of curses. The next day they met and the Messenger of Allah had a letter written for them to take back with them:

"In the name of Allah the Most Kind Most Merciful

This is the treaty that the Prophet and Messenger of Allah Muhammad has written for the people of Najran. He has determined that all their fruit, crops, their gold, their silver, their produce and their slaves would remain their property on condition that they pay two thousand sets of clothing; a thousand every Rajab and the other thousand every Safar."

Thereupon the delegation returned to Najran and on the way Bashir ibn Muawiyah decided to return to Medinah and embrace Islam as previously mentioned.

Jarud ibn al-Muala

Jarud ibn Al Muala was a Christian leader of the Banu Abdul Qays tribe. He came to the Messenger of Allah and said, "I have a religion. If I abandon my religion and enter your religion, will I not be punished on the Day of Judgement?" The Prophet replied to him, "This is correct." So Jarud embraced Islam becoming Muslim. The Prophet kept Jarud near to him due to his pleasure of his Islam. The famous Abu Huraira was the brother-in-law of Jarud bin Muala. Eventually Jarud settled in Basrah and was killed in Persia.

Jabr

(the freed slave of Bani Abd-al Dar)

Jabr the freed slave of Bani Abd al Dar was a Jew until he heard the prophet reciting chapter 12 of the Quran, Surah Yusuf which is mostly dealing with the life story of prophet Joseph. However when his master realized Jabr embraced Islam and became Muslim, he punished Jabr trying to force him to abandon Islam. Yet Jabr persisted upon the prophetic faith and methodology. After the conquest of Mecca, Jabr complained to the Prophet about the torture his master was putting him through. So the Prophet gave him wealth to purchase his freedom. Jabr thereupon earned his income from cleaning swords and utensils etc. Jabr became wealthy and married a woman from nobility of Bani Amr.

Jabal ibn Jawwal

Jabal ibn Jawwal was a famous Jewish poet who embraced Islam.

Jurayj the Israeli

Jurayj was a Jewish man who embraced Islam.

Durayd the monk

Durayd was a Christian monk, who became Muslim and was sent by Najashi from Ethiopia to the prophet. He was one of those who would cry profusely when he heard the Quran recited.

Dhu Mikhbar

Dhu Mikhbar was a Ethiopian Christian and actually the nephew of the Ethiopian King Najashi. He migrated to Medinah in the delegation Najashi sent to the Prophet and served the Messenger of Allah as a Muslim throughout his life. After the Prophet died then Dhu Mikhbar settled in Syria.

Dhu Mikhbar said:

I heard the Messenger of Allah say: you will make a secure peace with the Romans, then you and they will fight an enemy behind you, and you will be victorious, take booty, and be safe. You will then return and alight in a meadow with mounds and one of the Christians will raise the cross and say: The cross has conquered. One of the Muslims will become angry and smash it, and the Romans will act treacherously and prepare for the battle.

Zaid bin Sa'na

Zaid bin Sana was a Jewish Scholar.

Abdullah bin Salam narrates that when Allah decreed that Zaid bin Sa'na should accept Islam Zaid bin Sa'na himself said:

"When I looked at Muhammad, I recognized all the signs of prophethood except for two signs that I had not yet tested:

1. *That his self-control should outstrip his anger.*
2. *That his tolerance should conquer a display of extreme foolishness.*

Zaid bin Sa'na narrated that the Messenger of Allah had emerged from his room one day with Ali bin Abi Talib when a rider who appeared to be a Bedouin came to him. The Bedouin said, 'O Messenger of Allah! A few people from a certain tribe have accepted Islam because I told them that they will receive an abundance in sustenance if they accepted Islam. However no rain has fallen and they are afflicted by a drought. O Messenger of Allah! I fear that they may leave the fold of Islam out of greed just as they had entered out of greed. If you agree, we could perhaps send them something to assist them.'

Zaid bin Sa'na said, 'The Messenger of Allah looked at the person beside him who I assumed was Ali. He said, "O Messenger of Allah! I do not think that anything is left of that wealth." I (Zaid bin Sa'na) said, "O Muhammad! Do you wish to sell to me a fixed amount of dates from the orchard of a specific tribe (to be paid) before a specified term?" The Messenger of Allah replied, 'Alright but do not specify whose orchard it shall be.' Zaid bin Sa'na agreed and the deal was finalized. Zaid bin Sa'na opened his purse and paid 80 mithqal of gold for the specified amount of dates on a specified date. The Messenger of Allah handed the gold over to the Bedouin and said to him, "Take this to assist them."

Zaid bin Sa'na reported: When there were only two or three days left for the expiration of the term the Messenger of Allah left his house to perform a funeral prayer. With him were Abu Bakr, Umar, Uthman and several other sahabah. When they approached a wall to sit by it I (Zaid bin Sa'na) came to the Messenger of Allah and grabbed hold of his collar. I stared angrily into the face of the Messenger of Allah and said:

"O Muhammad! When are you going to pay my dues? By Allah! All that the children of Abdul Muttalib have learnt is how to procrastinate! By mixing with you people, I now have first-hand knowledge of this!"

As I (Zaid bin Sa'na) was doing this I noticed Umar's eyes were rolling with anger and he stared with fury. Umar said, "O enemy of Allah! Do you speak to the Messenger of Allah like that and treat him in this manner!? Had if not been for respect of being in the company of the Messenger of Allah, I would have cut off your neck!"

Yet the Messenger of Allah remained calm and unruffled. The Messenger of Allah said, "O Umar! All that the two of us need is for you to tell me to pay him quickly and to tell him to place his demands in a better manner. O Umar! Go with him and give him his dues. Also give him twenty Saa of dates extra in lieu of the threat you gave him."

Zaid bin Sa'na relates that Umar took him along, paid him what was due and added another twenty Saa to it. When asking Umar what the extra twenty Saaw were for, Umar said that it was the command of the Messenger of Allah because of the threat he(Umar) made. Zaid bin Sa'na said, "O Umar! Do you recognize me?" Umar replied, "No." Zaid bin Sa'na said, 'I am Zaid bin Sa'na.' Umar asked, "The Rabbi?" Zaid bin Sa'na said, 'Yes, the Rabbi.' Umar then asked "But why did you behave as you did? Why did you speak as you did?"

Zaid bin Sa'na replied, "O Umar! When I looked at Muhammad, I recognized all the signs of prophethood except for two signs that I had not tested:

1. That his self-control should outstrip his anger.

2. *That his tolerance should conquer a display of extreme foolishness.*

I (Zaid bin Sa'na) have now tested both these attributes. O Umar! I make you witness to the fact that I am content with Allah as Lord, with Islam as the true religion and with Muhammad as the Prophet. I also make you witness to the fact that I give half of my wealth – and I am one of the wealthiest people- as charity to the entire nation of the Messenger of Allah."

Umar said, "Say it is for a part of the nation because you will be unable to give all of them."

'Alright,' said Zaid bin Sa'na 'then for a part of the nation.'

Umar and Zaid bin Sa'na then returned to the Messenger of Allah and Zaid exclaimed "I testify that there is none worthy of worship but Allah and that Muhammad is Allah's slave and Messenger."

Zaid thereupon accepted Islam becoming Muslim and pledged allegiance to the Messenger of Allah.

Zaid explained his previously rude behavior: *"All the signs of Prophethood mentioned in Torah had been confirmed but only 'Hilm'- extreme tolerance of the Prophet in a situation where he is insulted and being humble towards ignorant even when someone tries to provoke his anger, remained. So I decided to check it out and now I am convinced that indeed you are the Prophet whose arrival is mentioned in our books."*

Zaid participated in many battles until attaining martyrdom during the battle of Tabook while advancing; before the retreat took place.

Aqib

Aqib was also a member of the Christian delegation that visited the Prophet from Najran. After they returned to Najran to inform their people about the treaty they secured with the Muslims then Aqib returned to Medinah and became a Muslim. His name before Islam was Abdul Maseeh which meant "Slave of the Messiah" so the Prophet changed his name to Aqib instead and had him stay in the home of Abu Ayyub al Ansari.

Abu Malik al Qardhi

Abu Malik al Qardhi was a Jewish Scholar from Yemen. He married a woman from the tribe of al-Qardhi; hence his name.

Umar ibn Khattab asked Abu Malik about the descriptions of the Prophet in the Torah. Abu Malik said:

"His descriptions are found in the book with the tribe of Harun. This book was neither changed nor altered. It reads, 'Ahmed, from the descendants of Ismael, appeared with the religion of monotheism, the religion of Abraham.'"

Abdul Qadus the Israeli

Narrated Anas:

A young Jewish boy used to serve the Prophet (ﷺ) and he became sick. So the Prophet (ﷺ) went to visit him. He sat near his head and asked him to embrace Islam. The boy looked at his father, who was sitting there; the latter told him to obey Abul-Qasim and the boy embraced Islam. The Prophet (ﷺ) came out saying: "Praises be to Allah Who saved the boy from the Hell-fire."

Source: Sahih Bukhari 1356

Ziyad ibn Shabtun, a companion of Imam Malik, stated, "The name of the Jewish youth was Abdul Qadus."

Adi ibn Umayrah

Adi bin Umayrah was Jewish and lived in a land dominated by Jewish monks. Adi died in Kufah in 40 AH. Adi related his reasons for becoming Muslim as follows:

"I found in the Book of Allah that the inhabitants of the highest level of Paradise are a people who worship their Lord on their faces. By Allah, I did not think this was anyone except for us Jews. And I believed the awaited Prophet would come from us. By Allah, it was not long before a man from the tribe of Hashim became a prophet. So I went to see him and found him, and those with him, prostrating on their faces."

Qays ibn Nushba as-Sulami

Qays ibn Nushba was well known for having read the previous Scriptures before the coming of the Messenger of Allah. When Qays heard of the Prophet, he came to visit the Messenger of Allah during the Battle of the Trench and said, "I am a messenger from my tribe, and they obey me. I will ask you some questions that are only known by way of revelation." Qays asked him about the seven heavens and those who reside therein. Qays also asked him about the earth. Finally Qays asked the Prophet what he was inviting the people to believe and do. The Prophet informed Qays about the teaching of Islam, its commands and prohibitions. Thereupon Qays said, "That which you call to is good, and that which you forbid is evil. I bear witness that you are indeed the Messenger of Allah." Then Qays returned to his tribe and called them to embrace Islam. Qays was well known as "the religious learned man from Bani Sulaym".

Maymoon ibn Yamin

Maymoon ibn Yamin the Israeli was a leading Jewish Scholar in Medinah prior to Islam. Maymoon recognized the truth of Islam and became a Muslim after meeting the Prophet. Maymoon then asked the Prophet, as head of state, to appoint him as a judge over the Jews. Maymoon said, "O Messenger of Allah, send them a judge from among themselves. They will be satisfied with me." However the Jews had yet to discover Maymoon became a Muslim. So publicly when the Jews heard of the appointment they declared: "We are pleased with Maymoon!" Thereupon Maymoon came out and declared, "I bear witness that he (Muhammad) is upon the truth and he is the Messenger of Allah." Although the Jews arrogantly refused to acknowledge this fact. So Allah revealed the following Quranic verse 46:10,

$$\text{قُلْ أَرَءَيْتُمْ إِن كَانَ مِنْ عِندِ ٱللَّهِ وَكَفَرْتُم بِهِ وَشَهِدَ شَاهِدٌ مِّنْ بَنِىٓ إِسْرَٰٓءِيلَ عَلَىٰ مِثْلِهِ فَـَٔامَنَ وَٱسْتَكْبَرْتُمْ إِنَّ ٱللَّهَ لَا يَهْدِى ٱلْقَوْمَ ٱلظَّٰلِمِينَ (١٠)}$$

Say: "Tell me! If this (Qur'ân) is from Allâh and you deny it, and a witness from among the Children of Israel testifies that [this Qur'ân is from Allâh (like the Taurât (Torah)], and he believed (embraced Islâm) while you are too proud (to believe)." Verily, Allâh guides not the people who are Zâlimûn (polytheists, disbelievers and wrong-doers). (10)

Abu Sad ibn Wahb

Abu Sad ibn Wahb was a Jew from the tribe of Banu Nadir. Abu Sad was one of only two men from this tribe to embrace Islam and faced severe social strains for doing so. The other Jew from Banu Nadir who became Muslim was Yamin ibn Umayr.

Saalba bin Qais

Saalba was a Jewish Scholar and his father's name was Qais. In Tafsir commentaries on the Quran Saalba is specifically mentioned as having 2 verses of the Quran revealed about him.

26:197

$$أَوَلَمْ يَكُن لَّهُمْ ءَايَةً أَن يَعْلَمَهُ عُلَمَٰٓؤُاْ بَنِىٓ إِسْرَٰٓءِيلَ$$

Is it not a sign to them that the learned scholars of the Children of Israel knew it (as true)? (197)

Ibne Abbas has narrated that once Hazrat Abdullah bin Salam۟, Hazrat Saalba۟, etc., came into the court of the Prophet۟ and humbly said O messenger of Allah, although we believe in you, the Quran, Hazrat Mosa, the Taurat, and Hazrat Ezra but do not consider it necessary to believe in other books and messengers of Allah too. Upon this, the verse of 4:136 was revealed:

$$يَٰٓأَيُّهَا ٱلَّذِينَ ءَامَنُوٓاْ ءَامِنُواْ بِٱللَّهِ وَرَسُولِهِ وَٱلْكِتَٰبِ ٱلَّذِى نَزَّلَ عَلَىٰ رَسُولِهِ وَٱلْكِتَٰبِ ٱلَّذِىٓ أَنزَلَ مِن قَبْلُ وَمَن يَكْفُرْ بِٱللَّهِ وَمَلَٰٓئِكَتِهِ وَكُتُبِهِ وَرُسُلِهِ وَٱلْيَوْمِ ٱلْأَخِرِ فَقَدْ ضَلَّ ضَلَٰلاً بَعِيدًا$$

O you who believe! Believe in Allâh, and His Messenger (Muhammad), and the Book (the Qur'ân) which He has sent down to His Messenger, and the Scripture which He sent down to those before (him), and whosoever disbelieves in Allâh, His Angels, His Books, His Messengers, and the Last Day, then indeed he has strayed far away (136)

WOMEN SAHABIYYAT

Safiyyah bint Huyayy

This great woman's name was originally Zainab but she is more famously known as Safiyyah bint Huyayy bin Akhtab bin Sa'yah and she was from the Jewish Israelite tribe of Levi and a direct descendant of the prophets Jacob, Isaac and Abraham. Safiyyah's bloodline is also traced to the Prophet Aaron through her father and to Prophet Samuel through her mother Dar. Safiyyah's story begins with a conversation she overheard between her father and her uncle:

"I was my father's and my uncle's favorite child. When the Messenger of Allah came to Madinah and stayed at Quba, my parents went to him at night. And when they looked disconcerted and worn out, I received them cheerfully but to my surprise no one of them turned to me. They were so grieved that they did not feel my presence. I heard my uncle, Abu Yasir, saying to my father, "Is it really him?" He said, "Yes, by Allah". My uncle said: "Can you recognize him and confirm this?" He said, "Yes". My uncle said, "How do you feel towards him?" He said, "By Allah I shall be his enemy as long as I live.""

Safiyyah's first marriage was to a Jewish poet named Sallam and they ended up divorcing. Safiyyah's second marriage was to Kinanah Abul-Huqayq who was also a Jewish poet. Her second husband was killed during the battle of Khaybar fighting against the Muslims. Safiyyah's father, uncle and brother were also slain during this same battle fighting against the Muslims. As a result of the battle of Khaybar, Safiyyah was taken captive as a prisoner of war and distributed as a slave to Dihyah al Kalbi.

However due to her noble lineage, her father being the chieftain and her beauty it was mentioned to the Prophet that she is only suitable for him and not Dihyah al Kalbi. So in exchange for Safiyyah the Prophet reportedly purchased her from Dihyah al Kalbi in exchange for seven other slaves.

The Messenger of Allah decided to marry her and her dowry was that he set her free from slavery. She readily sincerely embraced Islam despite her Father, Husband, Uncle and Brother having died in battle against the Muslims so soon beforehand. She loved the

Prophet deeply insisting that they journey away from Khaybar before consummating their marriage due to her fear that Jews might attack him. Years later when the Prophet was on his deathbed she said: "I swear by Allah, O Prophet of Allah, I would love that the illness which is afflicting you was inflicting me instead." After hearing this statement, the other co-wives of the Prophet looked at her and winked to each other. The Prophet said to them, "Go rinse out your mouths." They asked, 'From what?' The Prophet said, "From your winking to mock her, for I swear by Allah, she is surely truthful."

Safiyyah died in Muawiyyah's reign, she narrated several hadith.

A'ishah stated:

"I had never seen anyone cook better than Safiyyah. On one occasion, she sent some food to the Prophet when it was my turn to be with him. I was overcome by jealousy and broke her dish. Afterwards, I mentioned to the Prophet of my feeling much ashamed, 'O Messenger of Allah! What is the atonement for this mistake of mine?' He replied, 'A dish for a dish and food for food.'"

Narrated `Ali bin Al-Husain (from Safiya the Prophet's wife):

The wives of the Prophet were with him in the mosque (while he was in I`tikaf) and then they departed and the Prophet said to Safiya bint Huyai, "Don't hurry up, for I shall accompany you," (and her dwelling was in the house of Usama). The Prophet went out and in the meantime two Ansari men met him and they looked at the Prophet and passed by. The Prophet said to them, "Come here. She is (my wife) Safiya bint Huyai." They replied, "Subhan Allah, (How dare we think of evil) O Allah's Apostle! (we never expect anything bad from you)." The Prophet replied, "Satan circulates in the human being as blood circulates in the body, and I was afraid lest Satan might insert an evil thought in your minds."

Source: Sahih al-Bukhari 2038

Narrated Anas:

The Prophet stayed for three days between Khaibar and Medina, and there he consummated his marriage to Safiyya bint Huyai. I invited the Muslims to the wedding banquet in which neither meat nor bread was offered. He ordered for leather dining-sheets to be spread, and dates, dried yoghurt and butter were laid on it, and that was the Prophet's wedding banquet. The Muslims wondered, "Is she (Saffiyya) considered as his wife or his slave girl?" Then they said, "If he orders her to veil herself, she will be one of the mothers of the Believers; but if he does not order her to veil herself, she will be a slave girl. So when the Prophet proceeded from there, he spared her a space behind him (on his shecamel) and put a screening veil between her and the people.

Source: Sahih al-Bukhari 5085

It was narrated from 'Aishah:

that the Messenger of Allah became angry with Safiyyah bint Huyai for something, and Safiyyah said: "O 'Aishah, can you make the Messenger of Allah be pleased with me, and I will give you my day?" She said: "Yes." So she took a headcover of hers that was dyed with saffron and sprinkled it with water so that its fragrance would become stronger, then she sat beside the Messenger of Allah. The Prophet said: "O 'Aishah, go away, because it is not your day!" She said: "That is the Grace of Allah which He bestows on whom He pleases." Then she told him about that matter and he was pleased with her.

Source: Sunan Ibn Majah 1973 Grade: Sahih

Narrated Anas bin Malik:

We were in the company of the Prophet while returning from 'Usfan, and Allah's Messenger was riding his she-camel keeping Safiya bint Huyay riding behind him. His she-camel slipped and both of them fell down. Abu Talha jumped from his camel and said, "O Allah's Messenger! May Allah sacrifice me for you." The Prophet said, "Take care of the lady." So, Abu Talha covered his face with a garment and went to Safiya and covered her with it, and then he set right the condition of their shecamel so that both of them rode, and we were encircling Allah's Messenger like a cover. When we approached Medina, the Prophet said, "We are returning with repentance and worshipping and praising our Lord." He kept on saying this till he entered Medina.

Source: Sahih al-Bukhari 3085

Umm Ibrahim Mariyah the Coptic

Mariyah the Coptic was a slave of Muqawqis the King of Alexandria and Egypt. After receiving the Prophet's invitation to Islam, the Muqawqis sent Mariyah to the Prophet to serve him. Upon meeting the Messenger of Allah, Mariyah became a Muslim as did her sister Sirin. Mariyah bore the Prophet his son Ibrahim, but Ibrahim later died at the age of 17-18 months old; during infancy. Mariyah died during the Khilafah of Umar bin Khattab.

Narrated Al-Bara:

When Ibrahim (the son of the Prophet) died, Allah's Messenger said, "There is a wet nurse for him in Paradise."

Source: Sahih al-Bukhari 6195

Narrated Aisha, Ummul Mu'minin:

Ibrahim, the son of the Prophet, died when he was eighteen months old. The Messenger of Allah did not pray over him.

Source: Sunan Abi Dawud 3187 Grade: Hasan

Narrated Al-Mughira bin Shu`ba:

"The sun eclipsed in the lifetime of Allah's Messenger on the day when (his son) Ibrahim died. So the people said that the sun had eclipsed because of the death of Ibrahim. Allah's Messenger said, "The sun and the moon do not eclipse because of the death or life (i.e. birth) of someone. When you see the eclipse pray and invoke Allah."

Source: Sahih al-Bukhari 1043

Anas said:

We went in with God's messenger to visit Abu Saif the smith who was foster-father of Ibrahim (The Prophet's son who died in infancy), and God's messenger took Ibrahim, kissed him and smelt him. We went in to visit him later when Ibrahim was giving up his soul, and tears began to fall from God's messenger's eyes, whereupon 'Abd ar-Rahman b. 'Auf said to him, "You too, messenger of God?" He replied, "Ibn 'Auf, it is compassion," then shed more tears and said, "The eye weeps and the heart grieves, but we say only what our Lord is pleased with, and we are grieved over being separated from you, Ibrahim."

Source: Bukhari and Muslim

It was narrated that Asma' bint Yazid said:

"When Ibrahim, the son of the Messenger of Allah, died, the Messenger of Allah wept. The one who was consoling him, either Abu Bakr or 'Umar, said to him: 'You are indeed the best of those who glorify Allah with what is due to him.' The Messenger of Allah said: 'The eye weeps and the heart grieves, but we do not say anything that angers the Lord. Were it not that death is something that inevitably comes to all, and that the latter will surely join the former, then we would have been more than we are, verily we grieve for you.'"

Source: Sunan Ibn Majah 1589 Grade: Hasan

Narrated Jabir b. Abd Allah:

There was an eclipse of the sun in the time of the Messenger of Allah had died. The people began to to say that there was an eclipse on account of the death of Ibrahim. The Prophet stood up and led the people in prayer performing six bowings and four prostrations. he said: Allah is most great, and then recited from the Qur'an and prolonged the recitation. He then bowed nearly as long as he stood. He then raised his head and recited from the Qur'an but it was less than the first (recitation). He then bowed nearly as long as he stood. He then raised his head and then recited from the Quran for the third time, but it was less than the second recitation. He then bowed nearly as long as he stood. he then raised his head and then recited from the Qur'an for the third time, but it was less than the second recitation. he then bowed nearly as long as he stood. Then he raised his head and went down for prostration. he made two prostrations. He then stood and made three bowings before prostrating himself, the preceding bowing being more lengthy than the following, but he bowed nearly as long as he stood. He then stepped back during the prayer and the rows (of the people) too stepped back along with him. Then he stepped forward and stood in his place, and the rows too stepped forward. he then finished the prayer and the sun had become bright. He said: O people, the sun and the moon are two of Allah's signs; they are not eclipsed on account of a man's death. So when you see anything of that nature, offer prayer until the sun becomes bright. The narrator then narrated the rest of the tradition.

Source: Sunan Abi Dawud 1178

Rayhanah bint Zayd

Rayhanah was a Jewish woman from the tribe of Banu Nadir. Rayhanah was taken captive during the war and while initially she remained Jewish for awhile until eventually she accepted Islam. Upon her acceptance of Islam the Prophet offered to free her from slavery and to marry her. However she reportedly said it would be easier for her to remain a slave rather than become the wife of the Prophet as she thought it'd be mutually easier for her and easier for the Prophet. She died during the lifetime of the Prophet.

Khalidah bint al Harith

Khalidah was the paternal aunt of the famous and previously mentioned Jewish Sahabi named Abdullah bin Salam. Abdullah bin Salam's story related her embracing of Islam as follows:

"When I heard of the Messenger of Allah, I recognized his attributes, his name, and the time he would appear, which all coincided with our books. When he arrived in Medinah, a man informed me of his arrival while I was on top of my date palm tree. I shouted 'Allah is the Greatest!' My aunt was sitting beneath me and said " By Allah, if you had heard that Moses was coming you would not have been more enthusiastic." I said to her "O auntie, I swear by Allah, he is the brother of Moses who has been sent." My aunt said ' Is he the prophet that we were informed would appear during this time?' I said: "Yes." She said, "So be it." Upon the spot my aunt Khalidah bint al Harith embraced Islam as did my household.

Zaynab bint al Harith bin Salam the Israeli

Zaynab bint al Harith was the Jewish woman who infamously poisoned the Prophet with a roasted sheep.

Narrated Abu Huraira:

When Khaibar was conquered, Allah's Messenger was presented with a poisoned (roasted) sheep. Allah's Apostle said, "Collect for me all the Jews present in this area." (When they were gathered) Allah's Apostle said to them, "I am going to ask you about something; will you tell me the truth?" They replied, "Yes, O Abal-Qasim!" Allah's Messenger said to them, "Who is your father?" They said, "Our father is so-and-so." Allah's Messenger said, "You have told a lie. for your father is so-and-so," They said, "No doubt, you have said the truth and done the correct thing." He again said to them, "If I ask you about something; will you tell me the truth?" They replied, "Yes, O Abal-Qasim! And if we should tell a lie you will know it as you have known it regarding our father," Allah's Messenger then asked, "Who are the people of the (Hell) Fire?" They replied, "We will remain in the (Hell) Fire for a while and then you

(Muslims) will replace us in it" Allah's Messenger said to them. "You will abide in it with ignominy. By Allah, we shall never replace you in it at all." Then he asked them again, "If I ask you something, will you tell me the truth?" They replied, "Yes." He asked. "Have you put the poison in this roasted sheep?" They replied, "Yes," He asked, "What made you do that?" They replied, "We intended to learn if you were a liar in which case we would be relieved from you, and if you were a prophet then it would not harm you."

Source: Sahih al-Bukhari 5777

Reportedly Zaynab then became a Muslim after witnessing this miracle of the Prophet. However Bishr al Bara bin Marur al Ansari died as a result of the poison so some reports narrate that after her Islam the family of Bishr sought her execution as lawful retaliation.

Safana

Safana was the Christian sister of Adi bin Hatim who was left behind then freed by the Messenger of Allah and persuaded her brother Adi to go meet the Prophet in person. Her story was mentioned previously as part of the story of Adi bin Hatim

Seeriin

Seerin was the Christian sister of Umm Ibrahim Mariyah the Coptic, she also became Muslim as well.

Special Mention of Contemporaries of the Prophet

Najashi the Negus of Ethiopia

It was narrated that Umm Salamah, the daugher of Abu Umayyah bin al-Mugheerah and the wife of the Prophet, said:

"When we came to the land of Abyssinia, we stayed there under the protection of the best of protectors, the Negus, and we felt safe to practice our religion and we worshipped Allah without being bothered or hearing anything we disliked. When news of that reached Quraish, they decided to send two tough men to the Negus concerning us and to give the Negus gifts of some of the goods of Mecca. Among the goods of Mecca that he liked best was leather, so they collected a great deal of leather and they did not leave any of his bishops without giving him a gift. Then they sent that with Abdullah bin Abi Rabeeah bin al-Mugheerah al Makhzoomi and Amr bin al As, and they told them what to do. They said to them: Give to each bishop a gift before you speak to the Negus concerning them [the Muslims], then give the Negus his gifts, then ask him to hand them over to you before he speaks to them. She said: They set out and came to the Negus, when we were in the best land and under the best protection, and they did not come to any bishop but they gave him his gift before they spoke to the Negus. And they said to each bishop: Some foolish young men of ours have come to the land of the king; they have left the religion of their people and they have not entered your religion; they have invented a religion that neither we nor you recognize. The nobles of their people have sent us to the king concerning them, so that we can bring them back. When we speak to the king concerning them, advise him to hand them over to us and not speak to them, for their people know best about them and how to handle them, and they know best about their faults. They [the bishops] said to them: Yes(we will do that). Then they brought their gifts to the Negus and he accepted them from them, then they spoke to him and

said: O king, some foolish young men of ours have come to your land; they have left the religion of their people and they have not entered your religion; they have invented a religion that neither we nor you recognize. The nobles of their people, their fathers, uncles and clans, have sent us to you concerning them, to bring them back, for they know best how to handle them and they know best about their faults. Nothing was more hateful to Abdullah bin Abi Rabee'ah and Amr bin al-As than that the Negus should listen to what they [the Muslims] had to say. The bishops around him said: They have spoken the truth, O King; their people know best how to handle them and they know best about their faults. So hand them over to them and let them take them back to their land and their people. But the Negus got angry and said: No, by Allah, I shall never hand them over to them; I shall never expel people who came seeking my protection and settled in my land, and chose me over all others, until I summon them and ask them about what these two are saying concerning them. Then if they are as these two say, I shall hand them over to them to return them to their people, but if they are not like that, I shall keep them away from them and I shall be kind to them so long as they are under my protection. Then he sent for the Companions of the Messenger of Allah and summoned them. When his messenger came to them, they met together and said to one another: What will you say to the man when you go to him? They said: By Allah, we shall say what our prophet taught us and enjoined upon us, no matter what the consequences. When they came to him, the Negus had also summoned his bishops and they had spread their books around him. He asked them: What is this religion for which you left your people, and you did not enter my religion or the religion of any of these nations? The one who spoke was Jafar bin Abi Talib. He said to him: O king, we were an ignorant people, worshipping idols, eating dead meat, committing immoral actions, severing ties of kinship and mistreating neighbors; the strong among us would devour the weak. We were like that until Allah sent to us a Messenger from among us; we knew of his lineage, his sincerity, his trustworthiness and his dignity. He called us to Allah, to believe in Him alone and to worship Him, and to give up what we and our fathers used to worship of rocks and idols. And he commanded us to speak the truth, render back trusts, uphold ties of kinship, treat neighbors well, and refrain from crimes and bloodshed; he forbade us to commit immoral actions, speak falsehood, consume the wealth of orphans and slander chaste women. He instructed us to worship Allah alone and not associate anything with Him; he enjoined us to pray, give zakah, and fast – and he listed the commandments of Islam – and we believed in him and followed that which he brought. So we worshipped Allah alone and did not associate anything with Him. We regarded as forbidden that which he forbade to us and we regarded as permissible that which he permitted to us. But our people turned against us: they tortured us and tried to make us give up our religion and go back to worshipping idols instead of worshipping Allah, and so that we would regard as permissible that which we used to regard as permissible of evil things. But when they persecuted us and mistreated us, and tried to make us give up our religion, we came to your land and chose you over all others; we sought your protection and hoped that we would not be mistreated in your land, O king. The Negus said to him: Do you have with you any of that which he brought from Allah? Jafar said to him: Yes. The Negus said to him: Recite it to me. So he recited to him the beginning of Soorat Maryam, and by Allah, the Negus wept until his beard became wet and his bishops also wept until their books became wet when they heard what he recited to them. Then the Negus said: This and what Moses brought came from the same lamp. Go away, for we will never hand them over to you or harm them. Umm Salamah said: When they left his presence, Amr bin al-As said: By Allah, tomorrow I shall tell him of something that he will regard as serious, and by means of that I will be able to eradicate them. Abdullah bin Abi Rabeeah who was the more reasonable of the two men towards us, said: Do not do it, for they have ties of kinship with us, even though they have differed from us. [Amr} said: By Allah, I shall certainly tell him that they claim that Jesus son of Maryam is a slave (of Allah). Then he came to him the next day and said to him: O king, they say something very serious about Jesus son of Maryam; sent for them and ask them what they say about him. So he sent for them to ask about that. Nothing like this had happened to us before, so the people gathered and said to one another: What will you say about Jesus when he asks you about him? They said: By Allah, we will say about him what Allah said about him and what our Prophet said about him, no matter what the consequences. When they entered upon him, he said to them: What do you say about Jesus son of Maryam? Jafar bin Abi Talib said to him: We say about him what our Prophet taught: he is the slave of Allah and His Messenger, a Spirit created by Him and His word that He bestowed upon Maryam the Virgin. The Negus struck his hand on the ground and picked up a stick, then he said: Jesus son of Maryam is no different than what you said, not even as much as this stick. His bishops around him groaned when he said that, and he said: Even if you groan, by Allah! Go, for you are safe in this land. Whoever annoys you will be punished, then whoever annoys you will be punished, then whoever annoyed you will be punished. I would not like to have a mountain of gold in return for harming one of you. Give their gifts back to them; we have no need of them. By Allah, Allah did not take from me a bribe when He restored my kingdom to me, so why should I take a bribe to go against Him? And He did not listen to the people concerning me, so why should I listen to them and go against Him? So they left him, defeated and with their gifts returned to them, and we stayed in his land under the best protection. By Allah, we remained like that until some trouble befell him, ie, someone competed with him for his kingdom, and by Allah we never knew any grief or worry worse than that which befell us for fear that (this contender) would prevail over the Negus, and there would come a man who did not recognize our status as the Negus did. The Negus marched forth, and they were separated by the Nile. The companions of the Messenger of Allah said: Who will go out and watch the battle, then bring us the news? Az-Zubair bin al Awwam said: I will. He was one of the youngest of the people. They inflated a waterskin and he tied it to his chest, then he swam, floating with it, until he reached the other side of the Nile, where the people had met in battle. Then he went and watched them, and we prayed to Allah to grant victory to the Negus over this enemy and make him stronger in his land and give him full control over Abyssinia. We remained with him, in the best situation until we came to the Messenger of Allah when he was in Mecca."

Source: Musnad Ahmed 1740 Grade: Hasan

The Messenger of Allah also sent a letter to this Najashi with Amr bin Umayyah Dhamri which read as follows:

"In the name of Allah the Most Kind, the Most Merciful

From Muhammad the Messenger of Allah

To Najaashi Asham the king of Abyssinia

Peace be to you. Before you I praise Allah the Supreme Sovereign, Most Pure, Giver of peace and Protector. I testify that Jesus was the spirit that Allah created and His word that He cast to the chaste, pure and innocent Maryam. She bore Jesus whom Allah created from the spirit and breath from Him just as Allah created Adam by his hand and breath from Him.

I call you towards the One Allah who has no partner and to dutifully obey Him. I invite you to follow me, to believe in me and in that which I have brought because I am the Messenger of Allah. I have sent my cousin Jafar to you together with a group of Muslims. When they arrive, do treat them as your guests without arrogance.

I invite you and your forces to (the worship of) the Glorious and magnificent Allah. I have conveyed my message, given you good counsel so do accept my counsel.

Peace be on the one who follows the guidance."

Najashi sent the following letter in reply to the Prophet's letter:

"In the name of Allah the Most Kind the Most Merciful

To Muhammad the Messenger of Allah

From Najaashi Asham bin Abjar

May the peace from allah, His mercy and blessings be showered on you, O prophet of Allah. There is none worthy or worship but He Who has guided me to Islam.

O Messenger of Allah, your letter concerning Jesus has reached me. I swear by the Lord of the heavens and the earth that Jesus himself never said more than what you have mentioned. We understand the letter you have sent to us and we have entertained your cousin and his companions.

I testify that you are the true and accepted Messenger of Allah. I have pledged my allegiance to you at the hands of your cousin by whose hand I have accepted Islam for the pleasure of Allah the Lord of the universe. I am sending you (my son) Areeha bin Asham bin abjar. I have control over none but my own self. O Messenger of Allah! If you wish that I come to you personally, I am prepared to do so for I testify that whatever you say is the absolute truth."

Amr bin al-As related his story to Islam through a conversation with Najashi as follows:

"I used to be adverse and antagonistic toward Islam. I fought alongside the pagans in the battle of Badr, and I survived. Then I fought in the battle of Uhud, and I survived; and then I fought in the battle of the Trench, and I survived. So I said to myself, 'How many battles will I participate in!' By Allah, Muhammad will surely defeat the Quraysh. So I will take my wealth and go to al-What and avoid the people.

When the treat of al Hudaybiyyah occurred and the Messenger of Allah signed the treaty, and the Quraysh returned to Mecca, I started saying, 'Muhammad is going to enter Mecca with a tribe of his Companions. I have no place in Mecca or Taif. There is nothing better to do than leave, and I am far from Islam. In my view, if the tribe of Quraysh were to accept Islam – all of them – I would not accept Islam.'

So I went to Mecca and gathered the men of my tribe. They used to respect my opinion, listen to me, and put me forward to represent them. I said to them, 'By Allah, I believe the affair of Muhammad is going to overwhelm everything. So I have an idea.' They said, 'What is your idea?'

I said, 'We should go to an-Najashi and live with him. If Muhammad is victorious, we will be with an-Najashi. Living under an-Najashi is more beloved to us than living under Muhammad. And if the Quraysh are *victorious, then we are known to them.' They all agreed with this opinion. I said, 'Let's gather some gifts for him and the most beloved gift to him is leather.' So we collected a lot of leather, then we went to an-Najashi.*

By Allah, we were with him when Amr ibn Umayyah came. The Messenger of Allah had sent him with a letter he authored. And an-Najashi married him (the Prophet) to Umm Habeebah, the daughter of Abu Sufyan. He entered upon him, then he left. I said to my companions, 'That is Amr ibn Umayyah. If I go to an-Najashi and ask him to give Amr ibn Umayyah to me, he will; and then I will cut his neck. And when I do this, the Quraysh will be delighted, as I will have taken revenge against Muhammad by killing his courier.

I entered upon an-Najashi and prostrated to him like I used to do. He said, 'Welcome my friend. Did you bring me anything from your country?' I said, 'Yes, O king, I brought you a lot of leather.' I gave him the leather and he was impressed by it, and the rest we gave to the priests. When I saw he was happy I said, 'O king, I saw a man leaving from you, and he is a courier of my enemy. He has killed our leaders and notables. Give him to me so I can kill him.' This angered him, so he lifted his hand hitting my nose such that I thought it was broken, and my nose began to run. If the earth would have opened, I would have entered it to flee from him. I said, 'O king, if I thought this would anger you, I would not have said it.'

He said, "O Amr, so you ask me to give you the courier of a man who is visited by the chief Angel that used to visit Moses, and used to visit Jesus, so you can kill him?!'

Amr said, "So Allah changed my heart from what it was before and I said to myself, 'The Arabs and non-Arabs recognized this is the truth, and you are going to oppose it?!' Then I said, 'Do you bear witness to this , O king?' He said, 'Yes, I bear witness to it with Allah, O Amr. So obey me and follow him. I swear by Allah he is upon the truth. And he will be victorious over those who oppose him, just as Moses was victorious over Pharaoh and his army.' I said, 'Will you accept the pledge of my Islam?'

He said, 'Yes.' So I stretched my hand and gave the pledge of Islam. I came out to my companions, and I hid my Islam from them.

Then I left, intending to go to the Messenger of Allah and inform him of my conversion to Islam. I encountered Khalid ibn Waleed, and this was before the conquest of Mecca. He was heading toward Mecca. I said to him, 'Where are you going, Abu Sulayman?' He said, 'By Allah, I am getting on the road. This man is surely a prophet. I am going to him to accept Islam. How long will I delay it?' I said, 'As for me, by Allah, I only came for Islam also.'

We reached the Messenger of Allah and Khalid went to him first. He accepted Islam and gave him the pledge. I then went close to him. I said:

'Give me your right hand so that I may swear allegiance to you.' He held out his hand and I withdrew my hand. He said, 'What is the matter, O Amr?' I said, 'I want to stipulate a condition.' He said, 'What do you want to stipulate?' I said, 'that I will be forgiven.' He said, 'Do you not know that Islam wipes away all that came before it?'"

Daghatir

Daghatir was a Christian high priest and close friend/advisor of Emperor Heraclius. The Sahabi Dihya Kalbi was once sent with a letter from the Messenger of Allah to the Emperor of Rome. The contents of that letter were as follows:

"In the name of Allah the Most Kind, the Most Merciful

From Muhammad the servant and Messenger of Allah

To Heraclius the Emperor of Rome

Peace be on the one who follows the guidance.

I call you with the invitation of Islam. Accept Islam you will live in peace and Allah shall double your reward. However, should you turn your back, the sin of all your subjects shall be burdened on you.

"Say, 'O People of the Book! Come to (unite on) a word (a matter of belief) that is common between us and you; that we worship none other but Allah, that we do not ascribe any as equal (as partner) to Him and that we do not take each other as gods besides Allah. If they turn away then say, 'Be witness that we are certainly Muslims.'"

It is reported Heraclius told Dihya Kalbi "O dear! I swear by Allah that I know that your leader is the sent prophet and that he is the one we have been waiting for and who is described in our scriptures. However, I fear that the Romans will take my life. Were it not for this fear, I would have certainly followed him. Go to the high priest Daghatir and tell him about your leader for he is higher than me in status and more influential in Rome. When Dihya approached the high priest Daghatir and informed him of matters, Daghatir said: *"I swear by Allah that your leader is a sent prophet. We recognize him by his description and his name."*

Daghatir then entered his rooms and changed into all white clothing. Daghatir then went out to meet the Romans and testified that: *"I bear witness that no deity is deserving of worship except Allah and I bear witness that Muhammad is the Messenger of Allah."* The Romans immediately attacked and killed him.

Statements of Allah in the Quran about Ahl-Kitab Sahabah

وَٱعْلَمُوٓاْ أَنَّ فِيكُمْ رَسُولَ ٱللَّهِ لَوْ يُطِيعُكُمْ فِى كَثِيرٍ مِّنَ ٱلْأَمْرِ
لَعَنِتُّمْ وَلَٰكِنَّ ٱللَّهَ حَبَّبَ إِلَيْكُمُ ٱلْإِيمَٰنَ وَزَيَّنَهُۥ فِى قُلُوبِكُمْ وَكَرَّهَ
إِلَيْكُمُ ٱلْكُفْرَ وَٱلْفُسُوقَ وَٱلْعِصْيَانَ أُو۟لَٰٓئِكَ هُمُ ٱلرَّٰشِدُونَ

And know that, among you there is the Messenger of Allâh. If he were to obey you (i.e. follow your opinions and desires) in much of the matter, you would surely be in trouble, But Allâh has endeared the Faith to you and has beautified it in your hearts, and has made disbelief, wickedness and disobedience (to Allâh and His Messenger) hateful to you. Such are they who are the rightly guided, (7)

كُنتُمْ خَيْرَ أُمَّةٍ أُخْرِجَتْ لِلنَّاسِ تَأْمُرُونَ بِٱلْمَعْرُوفِ وَتَنْهَوْنَ عَنِ
ٱلْمُنكَرِ وَتُؤْمِنُونَ بِٱللَّهِ وَلَوْ ءَامَنَ أَهْلُ ٱلْكِتَٰبِ لَكَانَ خَيْرًا لَّهُم
مِّنْهُمُ ٱلْمُؤْمِنُونَ وَأَكْثَرُهُمُ ٱلْفَٰسِقُونَ

You [true believers in Islâmic Monotheism, and real followers of Prophet Muhammad and his Sunnah] are the best of peoples ever raised up for mankind; you enjoin Al-Ma'rûf (i.e. Islâmic Monotheism and all that Islâm has ordained) and forbid Al-Munkar (polytheism, disbelief and all Islâm has forbidden), and you believe in Allâh. And had the people of the Scripture (Jews and Christians) believed, it would have been better for them; among them are some who have faith, but most of them are Al-Fâsiqûn (disobedient to Allâh - and rebellious against Allâh's Command). (110)

۞ لَيْسُواْ سَوَآءً مِّنْ أَهْلِ ٱلْكِتَٰبِ أُمَّةٌ قَآئِمَةٌ يَتْلُونَ ءَايَٰتِ ٱللَّهِ ءَانَآءَ
ٱلَّيْلِ وَهُمْ يَسْجُدُونَ (١١٣) يُؤْمِنُونَ بِٱللَّهِ وَٱلْيَوْمِ ٱلْأَخِرِ وَيَأْمُرُونَ
بِٱلْمَعْرُوفِ وَيَنْهَوْنَ عَنِ ٱلْمُنكَرِ وَيُسَٰرِعُونَ فِى ٱلْخَيْرَٰتِ وَأُو۟لَٰٓئِكَ

مِنَ ٱلصَّٰلِحِينَ (١١٤) وَمَا يَفْعَلُوا۟ مِنْ خَيْرٍ فَلَن يُكْفَرُوهُ وَٱللَّهُ عَلِيمٌۢ بِٱلْمُتَّقِينَ (١١٥)

Not all of them are alike; a party of the people of the Scripture stand for the right, they recite the Verses of Allâh during the hours of the night, prostrating themselves in prayer. (113) They believe in Allâh and the Last Day; they enjoin Al-Ma'rûf (Islâmic Monotheism, and following Prophet Muhammad) and forbid Al-Munkar (polytheism, disbelief and opposing Prophet Muhammad); and they hasten in (all) good works; and they are among the righteous. (114) And whatever good they do, nothing will be rejected of them; for Allâh knows well those who are Al-Muttaqûn (the pious). (115)

48:29

مُحَمَّدٌ رَّسُولُ ٱللَّهِ وَٱلَّذِينَ مَعَهُۥٓ أَشِدَّآءُ عَلَى ٱلْكُفَّارِ رُحَمَآءُ بَيْنَهُمْ تَرَىٰهُمْ رُكَّعًا سُجَّدًا يَبْتَغُونَ فَضْلًا مِّنَ ٱللَّهِ وَرِضْوَٰنًا سِيمَاهُمْ فِى وُجُوهِهِم مِّنْ أَثَرِ ٱلسُّجُودِ ذَٰلِكَ مَثَلُهُمْ فِى ٱلتَّوْرَىٰةِ وَمَثَلُهُمْ فِى ٱلْإِنجِيلِ كَزَرْعٍ أَخْرَجَ شَطْـَٔهُۥ فَـَٔازَرَهُۥ فَٱسْتَغْلَظَ فَٱسْتَوَىٰ عَلَىٰ سُوقِهِۦ يُعْجِبُ ٱلزُّرَّاعَ لِيَغِيظَ بِهِمُ ٱلْكُفَّارَ وَعَدَ ٱللَّهُ ٱلَّذِينَ ءَامَنُوا۟ وَعَمِلُوا۟ ٱلصَّٰلِحَٰتِ مِنْهُم مَّغْفِرَةً وَأَجْرًا عَظِيمًۢا (٢٩)

Muhammad is the Messenger of Allâh, And those who are with him are severe against disbelievers, and merciful among themselves. You see them bowing and falling down prostrate (in prayer), seeking Bounty from Allâh and (His) Good Pleasure. The mark of them (i.e. of their Faith) is on their faces (foreheads) from the traces of prostration (during prayers). This is their description in the Taurât (Torah). But their description in the Injeel is like a (sown) seed which sends forth its shoot, then makes it strong, and becomes thick, and it stands straight on its stem, delighting the sowers that He may enrage the disbelievers with them. Allâh has promised those among them who believe (i.e. all those who follow Islâmic Monotheism, the religion of Prophet Muhammad till the Day of

Resurrection) and do righteous good deeds, forgiveness and a mighty reward (i.e. Paradise). (29)

5:83-85

وَإِذَا سَمِعُواْ مَآ أُنزِلَ إِلَى ٱلرَّسُولِ تَرَىٰٓ أَعْيُنَهُمْ تَفِيضُ مِنَ ٱلدَّمْعِ مِمَّا عَرَفُواْ مِنَ ٱلْحَقِّ يَقُولُونَ رَبَّنَآ ءَامَنَّا فَٱكْتُبْنَا مَعَ ٱلشَّٰهِدِينَ (٨٣) وَمَا لَنَا لَا نُؤْمِنُ بِٱللَّهِ وَمَا جَآءَنَا مِنَ ٱلْحَقِّ وَنَطْمَعُ أَن يُدْخِلَنَا رَبُّنَا مَعَ ٱلْقَوْمِ ٱلصَّٰلِحِينَ (٨٤) فَأَثَٰبَهُمُ ٱللَّهُ بِمَا قَالُواْ جَنَّٰتٍ تَجْرِى مِن تَحْتِهَا ٱلْأَنْهَٰرُ خَٰلِدِينَ فِيهَآ وَذَٰلِكَ جَزَآءُ ٱلْمُحْسِنِينَ (٨٥)

And when they (who call themselves Christians) listen to what has been sent down to the Messenger (Muhammad), you see their eyes overflowing with tears because of the truth they have recognised. They say: "Our Lord! We believe; so write us down among the witnesses. (83) "And why should we not believe in Allâh and in that which has come to us of the truth (Islâmic Monotheism)? And we wish that our Lord will admit us (in Paradise on the Day of Resurrection) along with the righteous people (Prophet Muhammad and his Companions)." (84) So because of what they said, Allâh rewarded them Gardens under which rivers flow (in Paradise), they will abide therein forever. Such is the reward of Al-Muhsinûn (the good-doers). (85)

3:199

وَإِنَّ مِنْ أَهْلِ ٱلْكِتَٰبِ لَمَن يُؤْمِنُ بِٱللَّهِ وَمَا أُنزِلَ إِلَيْكُمْ وَمَآ أُنزِلَ إِلَيْهِمْ خَٰشِعِينَ لِلَّهِ لَا يَشْتَرُونَ بِـَٔايَٰتِ ٱللَّهِ ثَمَنًا قَلِيلًا أُوْلَٰئِكَ لَهُمْ أَجْرُهُمْ عِندَ رَبِّهِمْ إِنَّ ٱللَّهَ سَرِيعُ ٱلْحِسَابِ (١٩٩)

And there are, certainly, among the people of the Scripture (Jews and Christians), those who believe in Allâh and in that which has been revealed to you, and in that which has been revealed to them, humbling themselves before Allâh. They do not sell the Verses of Allâh for a little price, for them is a reward with their Lord. Surely, Allâh is Swift in account. (199)

28:52-54

ٱلَّذِينَ ءَاتَيْنَـٰهُمُ ٱلْكِتَـٰبَ مِن قَبْلِهِۦ هُم بِهِۦ يُؤْمِنُونَ (٥٢) وَإِذَا يُتْلَىٰ عَلَيْهِمْ قَالُوٓاْ ءَامَنَّا بِهِۦٓ إِنَّهُ ٱلْحَقُّ مِن رَّبِّنَآ إِنَّا كُنَّا مِن قَبْلِهِۦ مُسْلِمِينَ (٥٣) أُوْلَـٰٓئِكَ يُؤْتَوْنَ أَجْرَهُم مَّرَّتَيْنِ بِمَا صَبَرُواْ وَيَدْرَءُونَ بِٱلْحَسَنَةِ ٱلسَّيِّئَةَ وَمِمَّا رَزَقْنَـٰهُمْ يُنفِقُونَ (٥٤)

Those to whom We gave the Scripture [i.e. the Taurât (Torah) and the Injeel] before it, - they believe in it (the Qur'ân). (52) And when it is recited to them, they say: "We believe in it. Verily, it is the truth from our Lord. Indeed even before it we have been from those who submit themselves to Allâh in Islâm as Muslims. (53) These will be given their reward twice over, because they are patient, and repel evil with good, and spend (in charity) out of what We have provided them. (54)

4:162

لَّـٰكِنِ ٱلرَّٰسِخُونَ فِى ٱلْعِلْمِ مِنْهُمْ وَٱلْمُؤْمِنُونَ يُؤْمِنُونَ بِمَآ أُنزِلَ إِلَيْكَ وَمَآ أُنزِلَ مِن قَبْلِكَ وَٱلْمُقِيمِينَ ٱلصَّلَوٰةَ وَٱلْمُؤْتُونَ ٱلزَّكَوٰةَ وَٱلْمُؤْمِنُونَ بِٱللَّهِ وَٱلْيَوْمِ ٱلْآخِرِ أُوْلَـٰٓئِكَ سَنُؤْتِيهِمْ أَجْرًا عَظِيمًا (١٦٢)

But those among them who are well-grounded in knowledge, and the believers, believe in what has been sent down to you (Muhammad) and what was sent down before you, and those who perform As-Salât (Iqâmat-as-Salât), and give Zakât and believe in Allâh and in the Last Day, it is they to whom We shall give a great reward. (162)

5:15-16

يَـٰٓأَهْلَ ٱلْكِتَـٰبِ قَدْ جَآءَكُمْ رَسُولُنَا يُبَيِّنُ لَكُمْ كَثِيرًا مِّمَّا كُنتُمْ تُخْفُونَ مِنَ ٱلْكِتَـٰبِ وَيَعْفُواْ عَن كَثِيرٍ قَدْ جَآءَكُم مِّنَ ٱللَّهِ نُورٌ وَكِتَـٰبٌ مُّبِينٌ (١٥) يَهْدِى بِهِ ٱللَّهُ مَنِ ٱتَّبَعَ رِضْوَٰنَهُ سُبُلَ ٱلسَّلَـٰمِ وَيُخْرِجُهُم مِّنَ ٱلظُّلُمَـٰتِ إِلَى ٱلنُّورِ بِإِذْنِهِ وَيَهْدِيهِمْ إِلَىٰ صِرَٰطٍ مُّسْتَقِيمٍ (١٦)

O people of the Scripture (Jews and Christians)! Now has come to you Our Messenger (Muhammad) explaining to you much of that which you used to hide from the Scripture and pass over (i.e. leaving out without explaining) much. Indeed, there has come to you from Allâh a light (Prophet Muhammad) and a plain Book (this Qur'ân). (15) Wherewith Allâh guides all those who seek His Good Pleasure to ways of peace, and He brings them out of darkness by His Will unto light and guides them to a Straight Way (Islâmic Monotheism) (16)

5:19

يَـٰٓأَهْلَ ٱلْكِتَـٰبِ قَدْ جَآءَكُمْ رَسُولُنَا يُبَيِّنُ لَكُمْ عَلَىٰ فَتْرَةٍ مِّنَ ٱلرُّسُلِ أَن تَقُولُواْ مَا جَآءَنَا مِنۢ بَشِيرٍ وَلَا نَذِيرٍ فَقَدْ جَآءَكُم بَشِيرٌ وَنَذِيرٌ وَٱللَّهُ عَلَىٰ كُلِّ شَىْءٍ قَدِيرٌ (١٩)

O people of the Scripture (Jews and Christians)! Now has come to you Our Messenger (Muhammad) making (things) clear unto you, after a break in (the series of) Messengers, lest you say: "There came unto us no bringer of glad tidings and no warner." But now has come unto you a bringer of glad tidings and a warner. And Allâh is Able to do all things. (19)

6:20

ٱلَّذِينَ ءَاتَيْنَـٰهُمُ ٱلْكِتَـٰبَ يَعْرِفُونَهُ كَمَا يَعْرِفُونَ أَبْنَآءَهُمُ ٱلَّذِينَ خَسِرُوٓاْ أَنفُسَهُمْ فَهُمْ لَا يُؤْمِنُونَ (٢٠)

Those to whom We have given the Scripture (Jews and Christians) recognize him (i.e. Muhammad as a Messenger of Allâh, and they also know that there is no Ilah (God) but Allâh and Islâm is Allâh's religion), as they recognize their own sons. Those who have lost (destroyed) themselves will not believe. (20)

98:1-8

لَمْ يَكُنِ ٱلَّذِينَ كَفَرُوا مِنْ أَهْلِ ٱلْكِتَـٰبِ وَٱلْمُشْرِكِينَ مُنفَكِّينَ حَتَّىٰ تَأْتِيَهُمُ ٱلْبَيِّنَةُ (١) رَسُولٌ مِّنَ ٱللَّهِ يَتْلُوا صُحُفًا مُّطَهَّرَةً (٢) فِيهَا كُتُبٌ قَيِّمَةٌ (٣) وَمَا تَفَرَّقَ ٱلَّذِينَ أُوتُوا ٱلْكِتَـٰبَ إِلَّا مِنۢ بَعْدِ مَا جَاءَتْهُمُ ٱلْبَيِّنَةُ (٤) وَمَا أُمِرُوا إِلَّا لِيَعْبُدُوا ٱللَّهَ مُخْلِصِينَ لَهُ ٱلدِّينَ حُنَفَاءَ وَيُقِيمُوا ٱلصَّلَوٰةَ وَيُؤْتُوا ٱلزَّكَوٰةَ وَذَٰلِكَ دِينُ ٱلْقَيِّمَةِ (٥) إِنَّ ٱلَّذِينَ كَفَرُوا مِنْ أَهْلِ ٱلْكِتَـٰبِ وَٱلْمُشْرِكِينَ فِى نَارِ جَهَنَّمَ خَـٰلِدِينَ فِيهَا أُولَـٰئِكَ هُمْ شَرُّ ٱلْبَرِيَّةِ (٦) إِنَّ ٱلَّذِينَ ءَامَنُوا وَعَمِلُوا ٱلصَّـٰلِحَـٰتِ أُولَـٰئِكَ هُمْ خَيْرُ ٱلْبَرِيَّةِ (٧) جَزَآؤُهُمْ عِندَ رَبِّهِمْ جَنَّـٰتُ عَدْنٍ تَجْرِى مِن تَحْتِهَا ٱلْأَنْهَـٰرُ خَـٰلِدِينَ فِيهَا أَبَدًا رَّضِىَ ٱللَّهُ عَنْهُمْ وَرَضُوا عَنْهُ ذَٰلِكَ لِمَنْ خَشِىَ رَبَّهُ (٨)

Those who disbelieve from among the people of the Scripture (Jews and Christians) and Al-Mushrikûn, were not going to leave (their disbelief) until there came to them clear evidence (1) A Messenger (Muhammad) from Allâh, reciting (the Qur'ân) purified pages [purified from Al-Bâtil (falsehood)] (2) Wherein are correct and straight laws from Allâh. (3) And the people of the Scripture (Jews and Christians) differed not until after there came to them clear evidence. (i.e. Prophet Muhammad and whatever was revealed to him). (4) And they were commanded not, but that they should worship Allâh, and worship none but Him Alone (abstaining from ascribing partners to Him), and perform As-Salât (Iqâmat-as-Salât) and give Zakât: and that is the right religion. (5) Verily, those who disbelieve (in the religion of Islâm, the Qur'ân and Prophet Muhammad) from among the people of the Scripture (Jews and Christians) and Al-Mushrikûn will abide in the Fire of Hell. They are the worst of creatures. (6) Verily, those who believe [in the Oneness of Allâh, and in His Messenger Muhammad) including all obligations ordered by Islâm] and do righteous good deeds, they are the best of creatures (7) Their reward with their Lord is 'Adn (Eden) Paradise (Gardens of Eternity), underneath which rivers flow, They will abide therein forever, Allâh will be pleased with them, and they with Him. That is for him who fears his Lord. (8)

5:54

يَـٰٓأَيُّهَا ٱلَّذِينَ ءَامَنُوا۟ مَن يَرْتَدَّ مِنكُمْ عَن دِينِهِۦ فَسَوْفَ يَأْتِى ٱللَّهُ بِقَوْمٍ يُحِبُّهُمْ وَيُحِبُّونَهُۥٓ أَذِلَّةٍ عَلَى ٱلْمُؤْمِنِينَ أَعِزَّةٍ عَلَى ٱلْكَـٰفِرِينَ يُجَـٰهِدُونَ فِى سَبِيلِ ٱللَّهِ وَلَا يَخَافُونَ لَوْمَةَ لَآئِمٍ ذَٰلِكَ فَضْلُ ٱللَّهِ يُؤْتِيهِ مَن يَشَآءُ وَٱللَّهُ وَٰسِعٌ عَلِيمٌ (٥٤)

O you who believe! Whoever from among you turns back from his religion (Islâm), Allâh will bring a people whom He will love and they will love Him; humble towards the believers, stern towards the disbelievers, fighting in the Way of Allâh, and never fear of the blame of the blamers. That is the Grace of Allâh which He bestows on whom He wills. And Allâh is All-Sufficient for His creatures' needs, All-Knower. (54)

24:55

وَعَدَ ٱللَّهُ ٱلَّذِينَ ءَامَنُوا۟ مِنكُمْ وَعَمِلُوا۟ ٱلصَّـٰلِحَـٰتِ لَيَسْتَخْلِفَنَّهُمْ فِى ٱلْأَرْضِ كَمَا ٱسْتَخْلَفَ ٱلَّذِينَ مِن قَبْلِهِمْ وَلَيُمَكِّنَنَّ لَهُمْ دِينَهُمُ ٱلَّذِى ٱرْتَضَىٰ لَهُمْ وَلَيُبَدِّلَنَّهُم مِّنْ بَعْدِ خَوْفِهِمْ أَمْنًا يَعْبُدُونَنِى لَا يُشْرِكُونَ بِى شَيْـًٔا وَمَن كَفَرَ بَعْدَ ذَٰلِكَ فَأُو۟لَـٰٓئِكَ هُمُ ٱلْفَـٰسِقُونَ (٥٥)

Allâh has promised those among you who believe, and do righteous good deeds, that He will certainly grant them succession to (the present rulers) in the land, as He granted it to those before them, and that He will grant them the authority to practice their religion, which He has chosen for them (i.e. Islâm). And He will surely give them in exchange a safe security after their fear (provided) they (believers) worship Me and do not associate anything (in worship) with Me. But whoever disbelieves after this, they are the Fâsiqûn (rebellious, disobedient to Allâh). (55)

www.ingramcontent.com/pod-product-compliance
Lightning Source LLC
Chambersburg PA
CBHW061707120626
46550CB00003B/1127